Contents

Preface

There are 3,000 different lan guages spoken by over 2,100 million people in the world, yet the World Tourism council that 80% of the world's tourism is organised using then English language. As tourism is becoming one of the largest industries in the world, and the international language of tourism is English, the aim of this dictionary is to give the users an insight into the essential words, phrases, abbreviations, acronyms, and factual information that are related to the tourism industry. This publication is not intended to be a 'in depth' reference book, but it has been published with different types of tourism needs in mind, such as students studying different types of tourism courses, and employees working within different sectors of the tourism industry such as tour guides, airline staff, hotel staff and travel agents, conference organisers etc.

We would like to thank many people who have helped with the publishing of this text: in particular Verité Reily-Collins, Alan Bowen and the ABTA staff at Newman Street, The Association of Independent Tour Operators, Valda Hurley of The British Airline Pilots' Association, the staff of Kensington and Chelsea library, David Leith, David Porter MSc., Jimmy Case, Ramsay Nassim.

Illustrations by John Cottier.

The front and back cover designs are by Emma Whiting.

Authentically English Dictionary For The Tourism Industry

Verité Reily Collins

Edited by David Leith

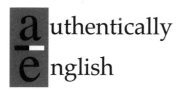

a uthentically
e nglish

Authentically English 1996

Publishd by Authentically English, 85 Gloucester Road,
London, SW7 4SS

Designed by Authentically English
Typeset by David Leith
Printed in United Kingdom by Aldridge Print Group,
Mitcham Lane, London SW16

International Phonetic Alphabet

At the beginning of each letter in the dictionary you will find the capital letter (upper case), the small letter (lower case) and the name of each letter in relation to the Phonetic/International Alphabet.

Throughout the world, all people that communicate by radio use the phonetic alphabet for transmitting information in order to aid clarity and accuracy. Flight numbers for airlines are an example for the need for clarity and accuracy. The flight number VS001 from London to New York (Virgin Atlantic 001) would be pronounced by air traffic control and the pilot 'Victor Sierra Zero Zero Wun'. This prevents any misinterpretation of the flight number that may cause dan-ger or any unnecessary confusion with other aircraft and their respective flight numbers. The letter 'V' could be mis-interpreted with 'D','B','C' etc, and also the letter 'S' could be misinter-preted with 'F', thus, the use of the phonetic alphabet. The numbers are pro-nounced in this way for exactly the same reason, and a list of the numbers is writ-ten at the end of this short piece.

Another very useful factor that the pho-netic alphabet has, is that it acts as a form of international communication due to it's worldwide useage. Different nationalities who speak different lan-guages can understand one another through this alphabet, as it is a global method for communication.

A	Alpha	U	Uniform
B	Bravo	V	Victor
C	Charlie	W	Whisky
D	Delta	X	X-Ray
E	Echo	Y	Yankee
F	Foxtrot	Z	Zulu
G	Golf		
H	Hotel		
I	India	0	Zero
J	Juliet	1	Wun
K	Kilo	2	Too
L	Lima	3	Tree
M	Mike	4	Fower
N	November	5	Fife
O	Oscar	6	Six
P	Papa	7	Seven
Q	Quebec	8	Ait
R	Romeo	9	Niner
S	Sierra	Hundred	Hun Dred
T	Tango	Thousand	Tousand

Dictionary for the Tourism Industry

The following section is the central part of the publication. Within this section, there are approximately 1800 words, phrases, acronyms and abbreviations with their definitions, that are directly relevant to, and associated with the travel and tourism industry. You will find some words have more than one meaning in relation to the industry, and this will be clearly defined in a numerical form. Each word will have either **v, n, adj** after it, that will describe to the user whether the word is utilised contextually within the travel and tourism industry as a verb, noun or adjective respectively. There will be many abbreviations and acronyms and these will be defined by **acr.** - acronym and **abbr.** - abbreviation. Finally, in the middle part of the dictionary, you will find seven line drawings that will illustrate seven different environments that are commonplace to the travel and tourism industry, with detailed word labelling of different items in the each of the seven different environments.

Abbreviations used in this dictionary.

abbr.	Abbreviation
acr.	acronym
adj.	Adjective
e.g.	for example
etc.	et cetera
Fr.	French
Ger.	German
i.e.	for instance
km	kilometre/
k.p.h	kilometres per hour
m.p.h.	miles per hour
n	noun
n.b.	Nota bene: note well
UK	United Kingdom
US	United States of America
v	verb

Aa - Alpha

A.A. (abbr.) Automobile Association (UK).

A.A.A. (abbr.) American Automobile Association (US).

A.A.C. (abbr.) Association of Airline Consolidators.

A.A.I.B (abbr.) Air Accident Investigation Branch.

A.B.A. (abbr.) Aircharter Brokers Association.

Abacus (n) CRS for airlines including Singapore International Airlines, Thai Airways and Cathay Pacific.

A.B.C. (abbr.) Advanced Booking Charter.

ABC World Airways Guide (n) Widely used airline time table and information guide. Published by Reed business publishing.

able-bodied passengers (n) Passengers permitted/requested to sit by emergency escape exits, who are capable of assisting with the evacuation of aircraft or ship.

Abonnement (n) European rail pass allowing the holder unlimited travel within a certain period of time (France).

abort (v) Emergency procedure. To stop an aircraft take-off when it has already started because to continue would be dangerous.

above-the-line (n) Advertising industry terminology. Advertising using traditional media including television, radio, magazines, newspapers and posters.

A.B.P. (abbr.) **1** Associated British Ports. **2** Able-Bodied Passengers.

A.B.P.C.O. (abbr.) Association of British Professional Conference Organisers.

abroad (adv.) In a country or countries other than one's own.

ABTA (acr.) Association of British Travel Agents.

ABTAC (acr.) Association of British Travel Agents Certificate.

A.B.T.O.F. (abbr.) Association of British Tour Operators in France.

A.B.T.O.T. (abbr.) Association of Bonded Travel Organisers Trust.

accessibility (n) **1** Ease of use of travel from one particular location to another. This can be measured by distance travelled, cost of travel, the time taken to travel, ease of transferring from one form of transport to another. **2** The level of ease or difficulty of access for disabled people.

accident insurance (n) Insurance carried by travellers to pay for emergency medical attention when away from their home country.

accommodation (n) Rooms that are provided for living and sleeping.

accompanying person (n) A person who accompanies a delegate to a conference, meeting or exhibition who does not attend any of the formal events with the delegate.

accreditation (n) **1** Official appointment or authorisation to act as an agent. **2** Authorisation for journalist to cover an event.

ACE (acr.) Association for Conferences and Events.

acknowledge (v) To let someone know you have received and understood their message.

acoustics (n) Relating to the quality of hearing or sound reproduction.

ACT (acr.) Association of Couriers in Tourism.

A.C.T.E. (abbr.) Association of Corporate Travel Executives.

act of God (n) Event caused by natural forces and beyond human control such as earthquakes, floods etc.

activity holiday (n) Holiday where guests take part in a sporting or other energetic activities.

A.C.T.O. (abbr.) Association of Camping Tour Operators.

A.D. (abbr.) **1** Anno Domini. Signifies after the death of christ, used in dates - i.e 1936 AD. **2** Air worthiness Directive. This is given when an aircraft has some defect that officials consider hazardous. The aircraft is not permitted to fly until the defect is corrected.

ad hoc (adj.) **1** Made by special arrangement. **2** When an interpreter translates conversation in a small group.

adaptor (n) Device that enables users of electrical goods to connect to foreign power supply outlets.

add-on (n) Additional or extra.

adjoining (n) Rooms that are next to each other.

admission charge (n) Fee payable in order to enter a venue.

adobe (n) Bricks of sun-dried earth or clay which are used as building materials.

advance booking/reservation (n) Booking prior to the start of a holiday.

adventure holiday (n) Holiday with a major sporting/activity content.

A.E.O. (abbr) Association of Exhibition Organisers.

aerodrome (n) Place where aircraft land and take-off. Smaller than an airport and mainly used by private aircraft.

A.F.A. (abbr.) Association of Flight Attendants (US).

affinity group (n) Special interest group.

affirmative (adj.) Yes.

A.F.O.R.R. (acr.) Association of Foreign Railway Representatives.

agenda (n) List of topics/subjects to be discussed at a meeting.

A.G.L. (abbr.) Above Ground Level.

agro-town (n) A town of population up to 20 000 people, with agriculture as the main economic activity.

A.I.I.C. (abbr.) Association Internationale des Interprétes de Conférence (France). International Association of Conference Interpreters.

aileron (n) Hinged flap at trailing edge of wings of an aircraft which move up and down to induce banking or turning.

A.I.P.C. (abbr.) Association Internationale des Palais des Congres.

Air Freedom Rights (n) Rights established for airlines by 1944 Chicago Convention. *First freedom* - to overfly one country en-route to another. *Second freedom* - to make a technical stop in another country. *Third freedom* - to carry passengers from the native country to another country. *Fourth freedom* - to carry passengers to the native country from another country. *Fifth freedom* - to carry passengers between two countries by an airline of a third on a route with origin/destination in its native country. *Sixth freedom* - to carry passengers between two countries by an airline of a third on two routes connecting in its native country. *Seventh freedom* - to carry passengers between two countries by an airline of a third on a route outside its home country. *Eighth freedom* - (Cabotage) to carry passengers within a country by an airline of another country on a route with origin/destination in its native country.

air hostess (n) Female who works on an aircraft serving passengers.

air miles (n) **1** Loyalty points earned by passengers by travelling on certain airlines, and also in exchange for buying some goods. Air miles, when redeemed give holders tickets for valid air travel. **2** Trading name of the company that administers points scheme for British Airways (UK).

air miss (n) When two aircraft unintentionally fly dangerously close to each other.

air pocket (n) Partial vacuum in air which can cause an aircraft to lose height suddenly.

air terminal (n) Airport building that provides services to passengers arriving and departing on airline flights.

air traffic (n) All aircraft in flight or operating on the manoeuvring area of a runway.

air traffic control (n) The official authority in charge of aircraft movements into and out of airports, and controlling aircraft movement in the airspace in their allocated zone or sector.

air traffic controller (n) Person working in air traffic control monitoring aircraft movements and giving instruction by radio to pilots to ensure that aircraft do not collide in the air or on the ground.

air waybill (n) List of goods or people being transported by air.

air-conditioned (adj.) Area cooled by means of refrigerated air.

air-cooled (adj.) Area cooled by a current of forced air.

airbridge (n) Corridor brought to the doors of aircraft to allow people to exit and to enter.

aircraft (n) Normally refers to an airplane (US) or aeroplane (UK), however, it can be used to describe any form of airborne transport.

aircrew (n) Pilot and other people on an aircraft who are needed to fly the aircraft and look after any passengers onboard.

airfare (n) Cost of a journey in an aircraft.

airfield (n) Small aerodrome, often privately owned, generally with no official presence - i.e. customs, etc.

airlane (n) Officially recognised route through the air used by aircraft.

airline (n) Company that provides regular flights for passengers or freight.

airliner (n) Large aircraft designed to carry paying passengers.

airpass (n) Special airfares for visitors from outside a country.

airplane (n) Aeroplane. Aircraft that has at least one engine and wings (US).

airport (n) Place aircraft land and take-off, that has facilities for passengers and often customs and immigration.

airport hotel (n) Hotel built on perimeter of airport, for use by air travellers.

airship (n) Large elongated balloon, containing a gas that is lighter than air which enables it to fly. Airships usually have a cabin to carry passengers beneath the ballon and an engine to power them.

airsick (adj.) Motion sickness caused by flying.

airside (n) area of an airport after check-in, that is between customs and aircraft - e.g. duty free shops are airside.

airspace (n) The air or sky above a country regarded as belonging to that country. Aircraft have to obtain permission to enter a country's airspace, as they would if they docked at a port or came in by road.

airspeed (n) Measurement in knots of

the speed of an aircraft through the air.

airstream (n) A current of air or a wind.

airstrip (n) A strip of land which is used by aircraft, often small private aircraft, for take-off and landing.

airway (n) Part or all of a controlled area in the form of a 'corridor' through the air. An airway has radio navigation aids throughout its route to help guide aircraft along it.

aisle (n) Passage between seating in an aircraft, train, theatre, church or at an exhibition.

A.I.T.O. (abbr.) Association of Independent Tour Operators.

à la carte (adj.) Menu providing a choice of separate items.

alarm call (n) Telephone or verbal message booked in advance, normally used to wake up a person.

alien (adj) **1** A person who is not a legal citizen of the country in which they live. **2** A person who belongs to a different country.

alight (v) Get down from/leave vehicle/transport.

allocate (v) Officially give out or assign seats, places or rooms.

allocation (n) Section, rooms, seats etc. reserved for a particular group or operator.

A.L.P.A. (abbr.) Air Line Pilots' Association (US).

alpine (adj) In, of mountains.

alps (n) Large mountains.

alternative tourism (n) Tourism designed not to damage the environment, that is 'ecologically friendly'.

altitude (n) The measurement in feet of the distance above sea level that a plane is flying.

A.M. (abbr.) Notation for the time between midnight and midday (morning).

Amadeus (n) CRS for airlines including Lufthansa, Iberia, Air France, Air Inter & SAS.

ambulance (n) Vehicle used for carrying sick or injured people to medical centre or hospital.

amenity kit (n) Complementary bag given out to airline passengers (usually Business or First Class) containing useful or luxury products designed to entice travellers to use the airline again. Often known as 'goodies bags'.

amphitheatre (n) Open-air theatre with rising rows of seats - often Greek or Roman.

amplification (n) Relating to increase in strength or intensity of sound.

A.M.T.A. (abbr.) Association of Multiple Travel Agents.

Amtrak (n) Railways organisation in the United States of America.

amusement park (n) Theme park or venue where visitors pay admission fee. May offer different forms of entertainment, including rides and other activities.

anchor (n) **1** A heavy hooked object that is dropped from a boat/ship/yacht to prevent it from moving. **2** (v) To prevent something from moving, keeping it in a fixed place (particularly associated with a boat).

animation slides (n) Projection technique which creates an illusion of movement when slides (photographic transparencies) are used in rapid succession.

animator (n) Person who entertains holiday-makers. (French)

Antarctic (n) Cold regions surrounding the South Pole.

Antarctic Circle (n) Line of latitude 66.5° South. South of which are the Antarctic regions.

anticyclone (n) An area of high barometric pressure, commonly several thousands of kilometres in diameter, with the winds blowing outwards, giving settled weather with few clouds.

ANTOR (acr.) Association of National Tourist Office Representatives.

A.O.A. (abbr.) Airport Operators Association.

A.O.C. (abbr.) Airline Operators' Committee.

A.O.N.B. (abbr.) Area of Outstanding Natural Beauty.

A/P (abbr.) Airport..

A.P. (abbr.) American Plan = full board accommodation, which includes meals.

A.P.C.O. (abbr.) Association of Pleasure Craft Operators.

APEX (acr.) Advance Purchase Excursion Fare. Ticket for air travel with limitations.

aperitif (n) An alcoholic drink that is served before a formal meal.

Apollo (n) CRS for airlines including United Airlines.

approach (n) Final part of a flight when aircraft is about to land at an airport.

approved (adj.) Agreed or endorsed.

approx. (abbr.) Approximately.

approximately (adj.) Near to correct or accurate.

A.P.R.O. (abbr.) Airline Public Relations Organisation.

apron (n) Area in front of terminal where aircraft park to load passengers.

A.P.T.G. (abbr.) Association of Professional Tourist Guides.

aquaplaning (adj.) When an aircraft skids on a wet runway at speed causing the wheels of the aircraft to lift slightly in the water, causing loss of grip.

aquifer (n) Rock which will hold water and let it pass through.

archipelago (n) Group of islands and the surrounding sea.

Arctic (n) Cold regions surrounding the North Pole.

Arctic Circle (n) Line of latitude 66.5° North. North of which are the Arctic regions.

area of outstanding natural beauty (n) An area, supervised by the relevant local authority, in which development is very carefully considered, so that the quality of the landscape is not diminished.

ARELS (acr.) Association of Recognised English Language Schools (UK).

armrests (n) Support for arms at edge of a seat.

arrivals (n) **1** Area passengers enter after disembarkation from transport and Customs clearance etc. **2** (adj.) People expected to or having recently arrived.

ARTAC (acr.) Alliance of Independent Travel Agents.

A.S.G. (abbr.) Air Safety Group.

A.S.M. (abbr.) Available Seat Miles.

assicuratione (n) Permit for Couriers to work in Italy (Italian).

assign (v) Allocate particular seat or workload etc.

A.S.T.A. (abbr.) American Society of Travel Agents.

A.T.A. (abbr.) Air Transport Association.

A.T.C. (abbr.) **1** Air Traffic Control. **2** Australian Tourist Commission.

A.T.D. (abbr.) Actual Time of Departure.

ATOL (acr.) Air Travel Organisers Licence.

atoll (n) a ring shaped island or a group of islands made of coral that has a lagoon in the middle.

A.T.S. (abbr.) Air Traffic Services. Organisation which has responsibility for flight information, alerting service, air traffic advisory service, air traffic control, approach control, etc.

A.T.T. (abbr.) Association of Tourism Teachers.

A.T.T.A. (abbr.) Africa Travel & Tourism Association.

attraction (n) Venue, place or tour destination that is of interest to visitors.

A.U.C. (abbr.) Air transport Users Committee.

audio conferencing (n) Discussion between three or more people in separate areas, who communicate using a telephone so each person can communicate. The practical maximum for this system is six people.

audio-visual aids (n) See **A.V.**

aurora borealis (n) Bands of coloured and white flashing lights seen in the sky north of the Arctic Circle.

authorise (v) To give permission to a person.

authorised (n) Officially appointed representative or officially aproved action.

autobahn (n) German motor/highway.

autocue (n) Reflecting sheet of glass in front of a speakers or lecturer, showing script which can be read, to give audiences the impression that they are not using notes.

auto-pilot (n) Mechanical means of piloting an aircraft, only used when plane is cruising and no major adjustments have to be made. Often known as 'George'.

autoroute (n) French motorway/highway.

autostrada (n) Italian motorway/highway.

A.V. (abbr.) Audio-visual aids are designed to accompany a speaker at a conference or meeting to help convey a message or lecture etc. Audio-visual aids include - film, video, slides, OHP, charts etc.

avalanche (n) A rapidly descending mass of snow, ice or rock down a mountain or the sides of a valley.

Bb - Bravo

B.A. (abbr.) British Airways.

B.A.A. (abbr.) British Airports Authority. Company that owns and operates some of world's busiest airports such as Heathrow and Gatwick.

BABA (acr.) Book a Bed Ahead (service offered in T.I.C.s).

baby-sitter (n) Person who looks after a child on behalf of the parents for a short time.

B.A.C.A. (abbr.) Baltic Air Charter Association.

back projection (n) System where an image is projected onto the back of a screen instead of from front.

back to back (adj.) When tour or charter leaves one group at destination while collecting the previous group.

B.A.C.T. (abbr.) British Association of Conference Towns.

badge (n) Identifying label or tag worn on clothes on which the wearer's identity is displayed.

baggage (n) Luggage, personal possessions packed in bags or cases for travelling.

baggage tag (n) Luggage label. Label attached to baggage etc. so that it can be identified.

B.A.H.A. (abbr.) British Activity Holiday Association.

B.A.H.R.E.P. (acr.) British Association of Hotel Representatives.

balcony (n) **1** A structure attached to the side of a building with a wall or railing around, it is situated above the ground floor to enable people to sit or stand in the open air. **2** The area of seating in a theatre or a cinema that is above the main seating area.

B.A.L.P.A. (acr.) British Airline Pilots' Association.

B.A.L.P.P.A. (abbr.) British Association of Leisure Parks Piers and Attractions.

bank draft (n) Cheque (check) drawn on a bank by a person. The amount of the bank draft must be paid in advance and therefore must be honoured by the issuing bank.

bank holiday (n) Statutory holiday during which banks are closed.

banquet (n) Large formal seated meal normally for a special occasion.

banqueting manager (n) person in charge of organising banquets, in an hotel or conference venue. They are responsible for the staff, supply of food and drink, maintenance, and finance of their department.

bail bond (n) Insurance document that covers payment for bail if a coach is involved in an accident (Spanish).

balance of payment (n) Amount still due on a bill or invoice.

balance of payments (n) The difference in a nation's economy between the income from the exports and the cost of imports.

bandstand (n) Round stage, raised above the ground, with a roof, used by bands when giving concerts outdoors.

banner (n) Long strip of cloth or material with a message or slogan written or drawn on it.

barbecue (n) Outdoor meal where food is cooked on an open charcoal fire.

bareboat charter (n) Yacht for hire without crew.

barge (n) Similar to a narrow boat that

is commonly seen in Europe. It is wider than a narrow due to the fact that the canals are wider in Europe than in U.K. - See narrow boat.

barman (n) Person who works behind a bar serving drinks to customers.

bartender (n) Barman (US).

barometer (n) Instrument for measuring atmospheric pressure used for predicting the weather.

barrage (n) A structure built across a river or estuary in order to slow or stop teh flow of water.

barrier reef (n) A coral reef stretching along a line parallel with the coastline but separated from it by a wide, deep lagoon.

BASI (acr.) British Association of Ski Instructors.

bassinet (n) Baby's bed or cot (US).

bastion (n) A defensive fortification which is part of a castle.

B and B (abbr.) Bed and Breakfast.

B.A.R.U.K. (abbr.) Board of Airline Representatives in the UK.

B.A.W.T.A. (abbr.) British Association of Wholesale Tour Agents.

bay (n) Part of the coast which curves inwards.

B-B-Q (abbr.) Barbecue.

beach (n) Area of sand or stones along the edge of the sea or a lake.

beacon (n) Marker or transmitter used for navigation. A system of navigational beacons transmitting on VHF, radiates a series of bearings. These are picked up on the aircraft's radio compass. Every time the aircraft crosses a beacon, the co-pilot reports the time it was crossed, height and estimated time for crossing the next beacon. The air traffic controller will not let the next aircraft cross that beacon until the previous aircraft is clear.

B.E.C.A. (abbr.) British Exhibition Contractors Association.

bed and breakfast (n) Accommodation providing bed and a morning meal, often in a private house (UK).

bed night (n) One person spending one night in accommodation.

bell boy/hop (n) Porter (US).

bell captain (n) Hall porter (US).

below-the-line (n) Advertising industry terminology. Advertising by direct promotion such as leaflet distribution, exhibitions, sponsorship and merchandising.

Benelux (n) Term for Belgium, Netherlands and Luxembourg, which is derived from their names.

Bermuda Agreement (n) Air service agreement between Britain and USA in 1946, relating to services between two countries, and often used as basis for other bilateral agreements.

Bermuda Triangle (n) A section of the Atlantic ocean between Florida, Puerto Rico and Bermuda, where aircraft and ships are said to have disappeared.

berth (n) **1** Place where a ship ties up or anchors. **2** Sleeping place on transport (ship, train etc.).

B.E.V.A. (abbr.) British Exhibition Venues Association.

beverage (n) Any drink except water.

B.F.H.G.S. (abbr.) British Federation of Hotel Guest House & Self-Catering Association.

B.H.A.B. (abbr.) British Helicopter Advisory Board.

biosphere (n) The area in which life exists on the earth.

bilateral agreement (n) Agreement between two countries.

bill (n) Statement of money owed.

bird scarer (n) Most airports have a member of staff whose job it is to keep birds away. If birds are sucked in to jet engines, they can do a large amount of damage and even cause accidents. Birds of prey are often flown to scare away smaller birds.

bistro (n) A small restaurant.

bisque (n) Fish soup.

B.I.T.O.A. (acr.) British Incoming Tour Operators Association.

black box (n) Slang name for the flight recorder on an aircraft. The flight recorder is actually in an orange colour box for easy identification, this contains records of airspeed, altitude, direction , vertical acceleration and flight time. Some boxes also record everything that was spoken in the cockpit, thereby, providing a record to an accident investigator.

black frost, black ice (n) A coating of transparent ice, not readily visible; hence its danger to road users and on runways, as it can cause skidding.

black economy (n) Black Market

black market (n) Illegal trading of goods.

black tie (n) Refers to bow tie worn with dinner jacket, but it now means that this is formal cloths are to be worn at function: dinner jacket for men and smart evening dress for women.

blizzard (n) Severe snow storm with high winds.

block booking (n) Reservation for more than one seat/room etc. booked at the same time.

Blue Badge (n) Term for British Registered Guides.

board 1 (v) To get on or into transport. **2** (n) Food or meals provided.

boarding announcement (n) Instructions given by airline employees to inform passengers when aircraft are leaving and when passengers board.

boarding house (n) Small house providing inexpensive accommodation, generally owner managed.

boarding pass (n) Ticket given to passengers to show that they have checked in. This ticket is presented by passengers before getting on to transport.

boat drill (n) Practice of emergency procedure on a vessel at sea.

body (n) The main part of an aeroplane, cylindrical in shape. Also known as the fuselage.

body language (n) Recognisable process of communication by physical actions or positioning of the body, rather than by use of words.

bonded (n) Tour operator that has lodged a sum of money and/or insured against losses to protect clients interests.

bonding (n) System of insurance which ensures that clients' money is safe once they have paid for a holiday, even if the tour operator ceases to trade. Major associations such as ABTA, AITO, etc. operate a bonding scheme for their own members.

book (v) To order or reserve something in advance.

booked up (adj.) Fully booked, no places available.

booking agency (n) Company that reserves theatre tickets, hotel rooms, transport, etc. on behalf of a client.

booking form (n) Voucher or document used to confirm a reservation.

booth (n) Soundproof small room or structure where simultaneous interpreters work.

Bora (n) A cold wind blowing down from the mountains on to the Eastern Adriatic coast.

botel (n) Floating hotel.

boundary (n) Imaginary line marking the limits of an area of land, a geographical region, economies or societies.

bow/bows (n) Front or forward end of ship.

box office (n) Place at a cinema or theatre where tickets can be purchased.

B.R. (abbr.) British Rail (UK).

brace (v) To stiffen one's body in preperation for a crash or an emergency landing.

brace position (n) Position of the body adopted to cause least injury when making an emergency landing.

break (n) **1** Interval for refreshment **2** Short holiday.

breakdown (n) **1** Mechanical failure of a vehicle. **2** Period of time after an exhibition closes when stands are dismantled.

breach of contract (n) Breaking a contracted agreement by not fulfilling all of the necessary terms and conditions.

break even (adj.) Amount of fare paying passengers needed to cover running costs of transport.

breakfast (n) First meal of the day.

break out session (n) Small group discussions held during a larger meeting or conference.

bridge (n) **1** The area of a large boat, ship, cruise liner where the Captain and his fellow crew pilot the vessel. **2** A card game commonly played on expensive holidays that are taken by older people.

bridle path (n) A path suitable for walkers and horses on which vehicles are not allowed.

briefing (n) Meeting to give instructions or information.

British Summer Time (n) National time in the UK in summer, one hour in advance of Greenwich Mean Time.

Britrail Pass (n) Train ticket giving

unlimited travel within a certain period of time (UK).

broad, broads (n) A series of shallow, freshwater lakes linked by channels found in East Anglia: known as the Norfolk Broads (UK).

brochette (n) Food on a skewer.

brochure (n) Leaflet or booklet giving details of an operator's holidays, prices, terms and conditions etc.

Bronze Age (n) Period of time about 4,000 to 6,000 years ago, during this period bronze, an alloy of copper and tin, was used to make tools and implements.

brunch (n) Meal combining breakfast and lunch served mid-morning (US).

B.S.T. (abbr.) British Summer Time (UK).

B.T.A. (abbr.) British Tourist Authority.

B-TEC (acr.) Business and Technical Education Council.

bucket and spade (n) A seaside holiday designed for children. Usually with sandy beaches so that children play in sand with a bucket and spade.

bucket shop (n) Company that sells tickets for air travel at very low prices.

budget 1 (adj.) Inexpensive. **2** (n) Estimate of money available and how it will be spent.

buffet (n) **1** A selection of food provided, from which guests help themselves. **2** A counter from which food is available at a station, on a train or ferry etc. (UK).

build up (n) A period of time before an exhibition or conference when staging and stand building takes place.

bulk clearance (n) When a group's luggage is cleared through customs together.

bulkhead (n) Dividing wall inside a ship or an aircraft.

Bullet Train (n) Japanese High Speed Train.

bumped (v) Off-loaded or denied a seat on an aircraft because of over-booking by the airline.

bunk (n) Bed built into a wall, usually in a ship.

bureau (n) Information office or travel agency.

bureau de change (n) Office where currencies can be exchanged.

business class (n) Airline class - in between Tourist and First class designed to cater for the business traveller.

business house (n) Travel agency that deals only with business clients.

business lounge (n) See executive lounge.

business travel (adj.) Travel for the purposes of work.

butler (n) In a large private house, the butler is in charge of the Dining Room, receiving visitors, and the other male staff. Some luxury hotels now supply butlers with executive suites, they are responsible for the comfort of specific guests.

buying forward (v) When a company buys foreign currency in advance of requirements.

B.V.R.L.A. (abbr.) British Vehicle Rental & Leasing Association.

Cc - Charlie

C (abbr.) Business / Club class on an aircraft.

C. (abbr.) Symbol for centegrade/ celsius.

C.A.A. (abbr.) Civil Aviation Authority

C.A.B. (abbr.) Civil Aeronautics Board.

cab (n) Taxi.

cabana (n) American/South American term for a small changing room by the side of a swimming pool. A cabana can be booked / reserved for private use.

cabin (n) **1** A room for sleeping and dresssing on a ship. **2** The seating area for passengers on an aircraft.

cabin attendant. (n) A member of an airline's or ship's staff who looks after the passengers.

cabin crew (n) Staff who look after airline or ships' passengers. United Airlines was one of the first airlines to introduce cabin crew. Their area manager, Steve Simpson, had the idea of employing crew members to assist passengers, and in 1930 these crew started work - and the idea spread. Today cabin crew have to be employed for safety reasons in the event of an accident. However, as they could fly for millions of miles before they might have to do anything, the airlines utilise their services to serve refreshments.

cabin luggage / baggage (n) Small hand-held luggage that passengers are allowed to take with them onto the aircraft.

cabin pressure (n) Air pressure inside aircraft cabin.

cable car (n) A vehicle for taking people up steep mountains or hills. It is pulled and suspended from a moving cable.

cabotage (n)

cafe complet (n) Continental breakfast with coffee.

cairn (n) A rough mound of stones piled up as a route marker, as a boundary indicator, or as a memorial.

call button (n) Switch which a passenger uses to call a cabin attendant.

camp (v) To stay or live for a short time in a tent which is out in the open air.

camper (n) **1** A person who partakes in the act of camping. **2** Short for camper van- vehicle in which people are able to eat and sleep.

Camp-site (n) An area outside in the open that has space for tents.

canal (n) An artificial waterway that enables barges or boats to travel across land. Also used for irrigation.

cancel (v) Withdraw, annul, call off, discontinue.

canyon (n) A deep gorge/ valley often with a stream or river.

capacity (n) The maximum amount allowed in a specific area, building or vehicle.

capital city (n) The most important town or city of a country or region due to the fact that it is usually the seat of government and the administrative centre.

captain (n) The person in charge of a ship or civil aircraft.

caravan (n) **1.**Mobile accommodation usually towed behind a car or horse. **2** A covered motor vehicle equipped for living in (US). **3** A group of pilgrims or merchants travelling together across a desert.

caravanserai (n) Place in Middle East where caravans, a collection usually made up of camels, stopped overnight. Now some have been turned into hotel accomodation.

cardinal Points (n) The major points on a compass: North, East, South and West

carnet (n) Official documentation or paperwork

carousel (n) **1**. A rotating conveyor machine that sends the passengers' luggage around the arrivals hall of an airport for collection. **2** Projector that has a slotted round drum situated on top that holds photographic slides.

carraige(s) (n) 1. The cost or the action of transporting or delivering goods. 2. The separate long sections of a train that carry passengers (UK). In the US they are called cars.

carrier (n) Airline.

carry-on bagage (n) Hand-held luggage taken by passengers onto aircraft.

cartel (n) Informal agreement of companies to maintain prices at a high level and also to control marketing arrangements. i.e. airlines, hotel companies.

cartography (n) The study and production of maps and charts.

cash bar (n) A bar, usually found at private functions, where the guests have to pay for their drinks

casino (n) A place where people play gambling games such as roulette. Can be found in hotels.

cassette (n) **1** A small plastic box. **2** A sound recording tape

catchment area (n) Region which has been covered.

caterers (n) **1** Company that provides food for events. **2** Staff who cook and prepare meals.

catering (n) Providing food or meals.

cave (n) A natural hole underground.

C.B. (abbr.) Continental Breakfast.

C.C.P.R (abbr.) Central Council for Physical Recreation.

C.C.T.V (abbr.) Closed Circuit Television (TV).

C.D.W. (abbr.) Collision Damage Waver. Agreement made when hiring a car. This means the hirer guarantees to pay the initial amount of money toward repairs etc. before claiming insurance.

centegrade (n) A measurement of temperature. Freezing point is 0 degrees centegrade, boiling point is 100 degrees centegrade.

C.G.T.B (abbr.) Canadian Government Travel Bureau.

chain (n) Group of hotels or shops that are owned or franchised by the same company.

chalet (n) **1** Alpine house especially in Switzerland. **2** A small house or hut on a beach or in a holiday camp.

chalet girl (n) A girl who looks after all the needs of guests staying in a chalet on the skiing slopes. Each day, the girl will clean the chalet, cook all the meals and generally look after the neeeds of the paying guests. She is usually employed by the tour operator who supplied the holiday to the guests, but some are employed privately by a specific family.

chambermaid (n) A woman who cleans and tidies bedrooms in a hotel.

channel (n) A natural or man-made water-course.

chart (n) Specialised maps used by airline and ships' navigators.

charter (n) Aircraft wholly booked for

a tour usually with no seats on sale to the general public.

chauffeur (n) The driver of a car that is employed to drive people around.

cheapie (adj.) Inexpensive ticket or tour (slang).

check-in (?) **1** Arriving at a hotel and going through the necccassary procedures to stay in tyhe hotel - i.e. collecting room keys. **2** Arriving at an airport and presenting your ticket etc. to enable you to to board a flight.

check-out (v) Leaving accommodation i.e. paying the hotel bill.

checklist (n) Printed list used to check equipment is present or working correctly.

chef (n) Person who is responsible for the kitchen and cooking in a restaurent or hotel.

chef du parti (n) Chef responsible for the operation of the kitchen in a hotel or restaurant.

child minder (n) See kiddies representative.

child seat (n) Small seat that is secured on top of a normal seat in transport so that children are safe while travelling.

Christmas (n) Christian Festival on December 25th each year. Celebrating birth of Christ.

Chunnel (n) Channel Tunnel - tunnel through which trains run providing a link between the UK and France (Slang).

chute (n) An inflatable rubber slide stored around the door of an aircraft for emergency evacuation.

circa (prep) About or approximately - usually refers to dates.

circle (n) Theatre or cinema seats in the lower balcony.

circular tour (n) Tour starting and ending at the same point.

C.I.T. (abbr.) Chartered Institute of Transport.

citizen (n) A person who has the legal right to live in the particular country of their birth.

citizens. (n) The people who live in a particular town or country. They do not necessarily have to be legal inhabitants.

citizenship (n) To have a legal right to live in a particular country.

C.I.T.O.G. (abbr.) Channel Island Tour Operators Group

CIF (acr.) Cost Insurance and Freight.

C.I.P. (abbr.) Commercially Important Person/Passenger.

city breaks (n) Short holidays based in a city.

claim (v) Demand for money as compensation.

claim tag (n) Small ticket given by airline, as a receipt, when checking in luggage.

clearing (n) Leaving i.e. Clearing Customs.

clearing house (n) An official or semi-official organisation which collects money, revenue and tickets and then distributes to members.

Clefs d'or (n) Society of Golden Keys - International association of top Hall Porters.

clientele (n) A group of clients.

climate (n) Normal or average weather conditions in a particular area or country.

cloakroom (n) Place where coats etc. can be left.

coach 1 A comfortable bus usually with only one deck (UK).

coach class (n) Economy Class (US).

coach control (n) Area where coaches wait at an airport or large venue.

coastal (n) By the sea.

cockpit (n) See flight deck.

cocktail lounge (n) Room or area where alcholic drinks are served and where seating is provided.

code of conduct/practice (n) Guidelines of the minimum standards for a group or association, which all members must follow or risk being asked to leave the group, i.e ABTA members have to adhere to the Association's Code, otherwise they are asked to leave.

code share (n) Alliance of different, sometimes competing airlines using the same airline prefix for agreed routes. Sometimes unpopular with passengers who do not know that they may not be flying on their preferred airline.

C.O.F (abbr.) Coach Operators Federation.

coffee shop (n) Inexpensive restaurant/ cafe in a hotel. Usually open throughout the day.

commentary (n) Talk given by Guide about a tour

commission (n) Money paid to someone for selling goods or services after the sale has taken place and the amount of which depends on the amount of sales - i.e. the more sales made the more commission paid.

companion way (n) Stairs between the decks of a ship.

compartment (n) Closed in seating area in a trains.

compass (n) Device for showing direction - an instrument with a magnetic needle which points out due North.

complain (v) To say that a person is not satisfied with something.

complaint (n) Reason or statement that a customer is not satisfied with something.

complimentary (adj.) **1** Given free of charge. **2** Giving praise or compliments.

comply with (v) To follow rules or instructions.

compulsory (adj.) Must be done or required by law.

concession (n) **1** Reduction in price of tickets for particular groups of people i.e. children or old age pensioners. **2** A space or rented area within other premises for running a small business or providing a service.

concierge (n) **1** Hall Porter. **2** Information desk clerk in hotel.

Concorde (n) **1** Supersonic passenger plane. **2** French hotel group.

conference (n) Meeting of people for discussions or exchange of information, usually held on a regular basis.

confidential tariff (n) List of prices only given to travel agents and tour operators, not to the general public.

confirm (v) To check or agree.

confirmation (n) Official agreement that something is correct or definite.

confirmed reservation (n) Booking that has been checked and the operator has agreed that there is a reservation.

congestion (n) over-crowded with people or cars.

congress (n) Large meeting or conference.

connecting passenger (n) Traveller who does not have a direct flight to their destination and has to change aircraft during their journey.

connection (n) When two transport services meet.

consecutive interpreting (n) Spoken translation of a speaker's words into another language, usually during a pause at the end of each sentence.

conservation (n) Protection of natural or man-made resources, including landscapes, buildings and their contents.

consolidate (v) Add together i.e. two

tours that haven't sold well will be combined because individually they will not be profitable.

consolidator (n) Person or Company that has agreement with an airline to sell excess capacity empty seats at lower than normal rate.

consul (n) Government official appointed to work and live in a foreign country to look after the interests of people from their own country travelling or living there. A consul can issue a new passport if one is stolen when abroad.

consulate (n) Official offices of the consul.

consultant (n) Professional advisor or expert.

consumer (n) person who buys products or services.

Consumer Credit Act (n) Legislation which regulates the provision of credit (loans, hire purchase etc.) allowing people who have made a credit agreement a period of time during which they may cancel it. This safeguards against high pressure sales techniques.

consumer protection (n) Legal protection for person who purchases goods or services so that they actually get what they have paid for.

continental breakfast (n) Small breakfast usually Coffee, bread rolls, butter and jam.

contraband (n) Goods taken out or brought into a country illegally.

conurbation (n) Marketing term for a heavily populated area where town boundaries merge.

convention (n) Conference (US).

co-pilot (n) The assistant pilot on an aircraft who is second in command to the captain. First officer.

corkage (n) Fee a restaurant/venue

charges if you provide your own wine.

COSHH (acr.) Control Of Substances Hazardous to Health.

costing (v) Process of obtaining true costs, goods or services for accounting purposes.

counter staff (n) Travel Agency booking clerk.

cot (n) Small child or baby's bed.

COTAC (acr.) ABTA/City and Guilds Certificate of Travel Agency Competence.

C.O.T.I.C.C. (abbr.) ABTA/City and Guilds Cert. of Tourist Information Centre Competence.

C.O.T.O.P. (abbr.) ABTA/City and Guilds Certificate of Tour Operating Practice.

C.O.T.O.R. (abbr.) ABTA/City and Guilds Certificate for Tour Operators' Representatives.

couchette (n) Small bunk or reclining seat on a train or a ferry designed to sleep in.

courier (n) A person who makes arrangements for, or accompanies, a group of travellers on a journey. Usually a Guide or Tour Manager.

cover (n) **1** A complete, individual place setting at a table. **2** The number of covers are the number of guests eating a meal at a function.

cover charge (n) Extras on a restaurant bill.

C.P.R. (abbr.) Cardio-Pulmonary Resuscitation. Emergency heart massage for first aid.

C.R.A.C. (abbr.) Continental Rail Agents Consortium.

crater (n) **1** Large hole at the the top or of a volcano. **2** Large hole in the ground caused by an explosion.

C.R.S. (abbr.) Central Reservations System.

creche (n) Children's nursery, where children are supervised where they can be left by their parents.

crew (n) Members of staff on an aircraft or a ship/boat.

C.R.S. (abbr.) Computer Reservation System.

cruise (n) Holiday based on a ship.

C.T.C. (abbr.) Certifield Travel Counsellor. Award of professional competence (US).

cultural tourism (n) Special interest tourism with art and historical tours.

culture shock (n) Cultural differences between countries or areas that cause travellers confusion.

currency (n) Money of a country.

customer (n) Person that buys goods or services.

customs (n) **1** Officials, usually based at a country's frontier, that are responsible for duty (tax) on taxable goods **2** traditional practices of a country or area.

customs officer (n) Official who works in the Customs area.

customs pass (n) Daily Pass issued to non customs staff meeting a flight at an airport i.e. issued to representatives of a tour operator.

C.U.T.E. (abbr.) Common User Terminal Equipment.

customer profile (n) An evaluation of a typical customer using a particular service or buying a particular product.

cut off (n) Time at which hotel/venue will no longer hold a reservation.

cut-off date (n) **1** Date when service finishes. **2** Date after which something is no longer being sold - i.e after the cut off date for a holiday no more bookings can be taken.

C.V.R. (abbr.) Cockpit Voice Recorder.

Dd - Delta

D. & D. (abbr.) Distress and Diversion (Air). Air traffic control sections for emergencies manned by Royal Air Force staff (UK).

dale (n) Name for a valley in Northern England (UK).

Danelaw (n) The areas of Northern England which were subject to Danish laws in the ninth and tenth centuries.

data protection (n) Ensuring that information stored on computer, usually personal, is not released to unauthorised persons or agencies.

Data Protection Act (n) Legislated act safe guarding the privacy of the individual by regulating the use and storage of information about people on computer (UK).

dawn (n) The first light at the beginning of a day.

day delegate rate (n) Special price offered by hotels to conference organisers, which includes meeting room hire, coffee and tea, lunch, etc. 24 hour delegate rate is all of this plus overnight accommodation, breakfast and dinner.

day hotel (n) Hotels built for short daytime stays often at airports or major stations.

deadhead (n) **1** Staff in transit travelling for free. **2** Transport travelling empty for relocation or positioning.

deck (n) The floor on transport such as boats/ships and buses. People are able to walk on them. Some transport has two decks such as boats, ships, double-decker buses and coaches.

deckchair (n) A folding chair that has canvas for the seat and also for the back. Commonly found on the beach (particularly UK), and on the decks of boats and ships.

declaration (n) Written statement made to a customs officer giving details of goods being brought into a country.

dehydration (n) Medical condition when the body has not taken in enough water to compensate for loss, through sweating, in a hot climate. Skin dehydration happens with air travel, where the skin dries out. Drinking water and using moisturiser helps to combat this.

delay (n) When transport or people cannot leave at the advertised time.

delegate (n) **1** Attendee at a conference. **2** Voting representative at an official meeting.

delta (n) Low lying area at the mouth (exit into the sea) of a river formed by deposits of soil or alluvium (sand or clay gradually deposited on a river bed). Normally a 'D' shape when viewed from above.

de luxe (adj.) High quality or a high standard of comfort. Luxury.

demi-pension (n) Hotel accommodation which includes bed, breakfast and one main meal per day.

demonstrator (n) Staff member, usually temporary, on an exhibition stand, who shows products to visitors.

denied boarding compensation (n) Payment by an airline to a passenger if they hold a guarenteed ticket and are unable to travel because the aircraft is overbooked.

departure (n) The act of leaving.

departure lounge (n) Room in which passengers wait before boarding aircraft, ship etc.

departure tax (n) Tax payable before leaving a country.

deposit (n) Sum of money paid to secure a room, ticket or seat, normally this is only a small percentage of the whole value.

depth markings (n) Numbering around a swimming pool showing the depth in feet or metres.

depressurisation (n) Emergency situation when the air pressure inside plane cabin drops rapidly.

deregulation (n) Removal of trade restrictions or controls.

descent (n) Downward path of an aircraft.

desert (n) Dry barren area with little or no water or vegetation, normally sandy or with very poor soil.

dessert (n) Sweet course or pudding eaten at the end of a meal.

destination (n) Place to which something or somebody is travelling.

devaluation (n) To reduce the value of a currency in relation to other currencies.

dew pond (n) Generally a man-made pond or pool designed to collect and provide water.

diner (n) **1** A person eating a meal in a restaurant. **2** A cheap restaurant (US).

dinner (n) Main meal of the day. In the US, dinner is a main meal served in the early evening. In the UK dinner is any meal served in the middle of the day, or a formal meal served in the early evening.

dinner jacket (n) Jacket worn, with a bow tie, by a man at formal social events. In the US this is called a tuxedo. When printed on an invitation it means men wear formal dinner jackets and women long or very smart evening dresses.

diploma (n) Qualification obtained by examination or assessment.

diplomat (n) An official representing a country abroad.

diplomatic bag (n) Container in which documents and goods are despatched to or from an embassy. Diplomatic bags are not usually inspected by Customs.

direct sell (n) Holidays sold directly to the public without using travel agents.

discount (n) Amount below the usual price - i.e. a deduction from bill or amount due.

discounted business/booking (adj.) Bookings or services given at a rate that is less expensive than the normal rate.

disease (n) Serious illness affecting a person or animal.

disembarkation (n) Leaving transport.

disregard (v) **1** Take no notice, ignore. **2** Radio communication term that means the previous message or statement was incorrect.

district (n) An area of a town or country that has official boundaries for the purpose of official administration.

ditch (v) Make a forced landing or intentionally bring an aircraft down on the sea in an emergency.

diversion (n) When a vehicle/plane is re-routed.

D.M.C. (abbr.) Destination Management Company. i.e. company that organises events for tour groups at their place of arrival.

document (n) Official paper or certificate.

dock (n) **1** An area of a harbour where ships and boats go to me loaded, unloaded and repaired. **2** (v) When a ship is brought into a dock.

Domesday Book (n) A survey of much of England carried out in 1086 by order of William 1 (William the Conqueror).

domestic (adj.) Internal flights or routes inside the same country.

domestic tourism (n) People taking holidays in their own country.

doorman (n) Uniformed member of staff on duty at the entrance of a hotel or grand venue, who opens car doors, shelters you with umbrella, etc.

double-decker (n) Bus/coach with an upper and lower floor for carrying passengers.

double occupancy (n) Two people sharing one bedroom.

Dollar (n) Unit of currency (Australia, N.Z., U.S. etc.) said to derive name from old Austrian coin, the Thaler.

dormitory (n) Room for sleeping in, containing a number of beds. Usually for young people.

D.o.T. (abbr.) Department of Transportation (U.S).

down market (n) Inexpensive or inferior.

downgrade (v) Move to less expensive or inferior seats or accommodation.

downtown (adj) The centre of a town or city (US).

drag (n) Air resistance on an aircraft or other vehicle.

driver (n) Person who drives a taxi, coach or other road vehicle.

drivers' hours (n) The legal length of time that a coach or bus driver is allowed to drive per day.

dry goods/stores (n) Tea, coffee, sugar and other powdered goods that will not spoil for a long time.

dry lease (n) Where an aircraft is leased without an aircrew.

dupe (abbr.) Duplicate. Term used when there are too many passengers for a regular bus or coach service. This means that an additional coach or bus (dupe) will need to be provided in order to transport the additional passengers.

duplex (n) Hotel suite that has two floors that are connected by an internal stairway.

dusk (n) The time of the day when the light is disappearing, but it is not completely dark.

duty (n) **1** Work schedule or roster - On Duty = working; Off Duty = not working. **2** Tax on certain goods being brought into a country.

duty free (n) Goods that are sold free of taxes.

duty manager/ officer (n) Manager/ officer who is on duty or in charge at a certain time.

duty rota (n) Plan of staff working hours and shifts.

duvet (n) Bedcover filled with feathers, down, or foam, used in most European hotels.

D.W.B. (abbr.) Double With Bathroom. Double bedded room with an en-suite bathroom.

Ee - Echo

E (abbr.) Estimated.

E111 (n) Number of the form provided by Department of Health which entitles British nationals too free medical attention in countries that have arrangements with the British government (UK).

earphones (n) Covers for ears which have small electronic speakers in them so that people can listen to sound without sisturbing anybody else - i.e. for simultaneous translation or to listen to In-flight entertainment.

ear plugs (n) Pieces of soft foam which can be inserted in ear to keep out noise.

earthquake (n) A sudden violent movement of the Earth's surface, often causing great damage.

Easter (n) Annual Christian religous festival that takes place in March or April. Traditionally the start to European summer season.

E.A.T.A. (abbr.) East Asia Travel Association.

ebb (n) Water flowing away from the land - i.e. ebb tide.

E.C. (abbr.) European Community

eco- Prefix to words generally relating to protection of the environment i.e. Ecology, Ecosystem.

ecology (n) Study of plants and animals in relation to each other and their natural enviroment.

economy class (n) Tourist class seats in an aircraft.

ecosystem (n) Collection of plants and animals that live within a particular physical environment.

E.C.T.A.A. (abbr.) European Community Travel Agents and tour operators Association

ECU (acr.) European Currency Unit

educational (n) Organised visit where Travel Agents, Conference Organisers or the Press are invited to visit an area, a group of hotels, or place of interest. The object being to display the venues so that they will gain more business or publicity.

educational visit (n) Tour to a work place or factory which is topically relevant to conference, etc.

E.F.A.H. (abbr.) European Foundation for the Accreditation of Hotel school programmes

E.F.C.T. (abbr.) European Federation of Conference Towns

E.F.T.A. (abbr.) European Free Trade Association currently comprises of many European countries that are not members of the E.U.

E.H.O. (abbr.) Environmental Health Officer. Official paid by local council to investigate health and safety matters in a borough or area.

E.I.A. (abbr.) Environmental Impact Assessment. To measure the probable results of human intervention on the environment

elapsed flying time (n) Actual time spent on a flight between two places.

elbow (n) Fare paid on transport to a crew member who keeps the payment.

electric Supply (n) Socket or outlet from which electricity can be taken. This varies around the world - usually it is either 120 volts or 220/240. n.b. Never let travellers use the wrong plug or appliance for the local voltage as this can be dangerous.

electronic mail (n) Transfer of written

information or images by means of computers linked by telephone to a central network.

electronic payment (n) Payment by means of electronic transfer rather than cash or cheque.

elevator (n) **1** See Lift (UK). **2** Horizontal control surfaces on the wings of an aircraft used to control climbing and descent.

email (n) See electronic mail.

embargo (n) Official ban on trade, this can include imports, flights or information.

embark (v) To go on board an aircraft or ship.

embarkation (n) Place or area at which a person embarks or leaves.

embarkation card (n) See boarding pass.

embassy (n) Official offices of a the Ambassador in a foreign country.

emergency (n) A sudden serious situation or event that needs immediate action or attention.

emergency aid (n) First aid.

emergency card (n) Leaflet kept in the pocket of an aircraft seat, giving safety instructions.

emergency exit (n) Door designated as way out in the event of fire or any other emergency.

emergency landing (n) When an aircraft has to make a sudden, unplanned landing because of an emergency.

empty leg (n) Journey made with no passengers on board, usually when locating coach or plane at the start or end of a tour or season

empty run (n) See empty leg.

endorsement (n) Official approval to support a claim, statement or course of action.

English breakfast (n) Cooked breakfast, with fried eggs, bacon and sausages etc.

English Channel (n) Stretch of water separating the United Kingdom from France.

en pension (n) Accommodation with meal/s.

entrée (n) Food dish that forms main course of a meal.

environment (n) surrounding area, especially an area in which people or animals live or work.

environmental hazard (n) Natural danger - i.e. earthquake, flood, volcanic eruption or drought.

environmentally sensitive area (n) Area with a fragile ecosystem which will only be maintained by conscious attempts to protect it.

E.P.O.S. (abbr.) Electronic Point of Sale.

E.P.S. (abbr.) European Passenger Services.

equator (n) Imaginary line around the centre of the world at an equal distance between the South and North Poles.

equatorial current (n) The surface movement of ocean currents near the equator.

equinox (n) One of the two days in the year when the day and night are of equal length. This normally happens around March 20 and September 20.

E.R.M. (abbr.) Exchange Rate Mechanism (European).

erosion (n) Gradual destruction of rock or soil by rain, wind, sea, ice.

escalator (n) A moving stairway/staircase that enables people to travel from one floor to another within a building or station.

escort (n) Term for a courier or represemntative, not often used except by the British Foreign Office (government department in the UK) and by traditional travel companies.

escorted tours (n) Tours accompanied by a leader.

escrow (n) Arrangement where payment for a service or goods is held in a seperate bank account or by an organisation not involved in the transaction. The payment is not transferred until the service or goods have been supplied.

E.S.I.T.O. (abbr.) Events Sector Industry Training Association

estimate (n) approximate calculation or amount.

estuary (n) Wide area of a river where it joins the sea.

E.T.A. (abbr.) Estimated Time of Arrival.

E.T.B. (abbr.) English Tourist Board.

E.T.D. (abbr.) Estimated Time of Departure.

ethnic traffic (n) Travellers from a particular racial group.

E.T.O.A. (abbr.) European Tour Operators Association.

E.U. (abbr.) European Union.

Euroline (n) Company that runs a network of coach services across Europe.

european plan (n) Hotel rate for accommodation only.

Eurostar (n) Train connecting the UK with France through the channel tunnel.

Eurotunnel (n) Tunnel under Channel connecting France and the UK.

evacuate (v) To leave an area of danger quickly.

evacuation slide (n) Inflatable slide or chute, usually stored around door of an aircraft. The slide inflates in the event of an emergency, so people can use it to leave the aircraft quickly.

everglades (n) wetlands in Florida with small islands.

excess luggage (n) More luggage than

allowed for in the ticket price. Usually carried at an extra charge.

exchange rate (n) Value of one currency compared to other currencies.

excursion (n) Short journey or visit made by people for pleasure.

excursion fare (n) Promotional fare offering a special low rate, often with a minimum or maximum stay requirement.

excursionist (n) Official term for a visitor to a country who stays for less than 24 hours.

executive club (n) **1** Private lounge at an airport reserved for VIPs and business travellers of an airline. **2** British Airways VIP Lounge.

executive lounge (n) A large room at airports and railway stations for specific travellers. These travellers could be guests of the airline, commercially important or members of an airline club.

exempt (adj.) Free from duty or payment.

exhibition (n) Event or fair where companies or people display or show things.

exhibitors' pass (n) Identification card for people who have a stand at an exhibition to gain access to the exhibition.

exit (n) Way out.

expenditure (n) Money paid out or spent.

expenses (n) Money paid out by an to staff to cover any costs staff incur while working - i.e. food and transport costs.

expiry date (n) Date after which something is no longer valid - i.e. a ticket.

export bureau (n) Office in a large shop or store that advises on the reclaiming of local taxes on goods purchased and also the shipping of goods purchased.

extend (v) Make longer or prolong i.e to on holiday longer than planned.

extras (n) Bill for items that are not included in the price usually at a hotel.

external checks (v) Checks a pilot makes before take-off in an aircraft.

Ff - Foxtrot

F (abbr.) **1** First class. **2** Symbol for fahrenheit.

F.A.A. (abbr.) Federal Aviation Authority (US).

facility (n) Any item or any service provided at a venue to add to a visitor's pleasure or convenience.

facilitator (n) Person who makes something easier to do.

fair (n) **1** Large exhibition to promote business or visitors to a town or city. **2** A market or show with entertainments held regularly in the same place usually outdoors.

FAM. TRIP (abbr.) Familiarisation Trip. Trip organised to promote an area or venue to prospective users.

family cabin (n) Cabin with four or more berths.

Fantasia (n) CRS for airlines including JAL and Qantas.

fahrenheit (n) A measurement of temperature. Freezing point is 32 degrees fahrenheit, boiling point is 212 degrees fahrenheit.

fare (n) The cost of travelling by transport from one destination to another.

farm tourism (n) Holiday where visitors stay on a farm.

fast food (n) Hot food that can be purchased quickly and eaten in a shop or restaurant, and that can also be taken out and eaten whilst travelling or walking e.g. fish and chips, hamburger, hot dog etc.

Far East (n) Referring to the countries of Eastern Asia including China, North and South Korea and Japan.

Fast Track (n) Initiative of B.A.A. to allow passengers that pay a premium through airport formalities quicker than other travellers.

fathom (n) Nautical measurement of depth. 1 fathom = 6 feet or approximately 2 metres.

fax (n) Facsimile machine. Machine that can transmit copies of letters, documents and illustrations electronically using telephone lines to other fax machines.

feedback (n) Comments from passengers or customers about products or services that they have used.

fens (n) Low lying wetlands in East Anglia (UK).

ferry (n) Boat or ship that carries people and/or vehicles across an area of water.

festival (n) Organised series of events, generally music, drama or dance performances taking place during a specific week or days.

F.I.A.V.E.T. (abbr.) Federazione Italiana del Associazioni Turistici.

field trip (n) Journey made in order to study or reasearch something in a practical way.

fiesta (n) Public holiday or celebration, especially a religious holiday.

filler (n) Short story or anecdote to fill in a pause during a commentary.

fine (n) Payment of money, as punishment for breaking the law.

final approach (n) Last four miles of the approach to an airport by an aircraft during which time the aircraft is in a direct line with the runway for landing.

fiord, fjord (n) A long narrow strip of the sea leading into the interior of a country.

fire exit (n) Way out or escape in the event of fire. By law these must be available in all public places, and must not be obstructed.

fire extinguisher (n) Canister containing water or chemicals which can be sprayed on a fire to put it out.

first aid (n) Medical attention or help given to an injured person before they are seen by a doctor or taken to a hospital.

first aid kit (n) See Medical Kit.

first class (n) Most expensive and the most comfortable area or cabins in a train, ship or aircraft.

first officer (n) Officer who is the assistant to the captain, usually second in command, on a ship or an aircraft. See also co- pilot.

fissure (n) A long deep crack in earth or rock.

F.I.T. (abbr.) Fully inclusive tour for Independent Travellers.

F.I.S. (abbr.) Flight Information Service.

flag (n) Piece of cloth which has a design or logo on it that represents a particular country or organisation. These are often tied to a pole down one edge and allowed to be blown by the wind.

flag carrier (n) National airline of a particular country.

flag of convenience (n) Flag of a country under which a ship registers, so that the owner of the ship can avoid paying the taxes or reguations of their home country.

flaps (n) Moving parts on the wing of an aircraft to increase lift and/or drag.

flash flood (n) A sudden flood caused by heavy rain.

flight (n) Journey by air in an aircraft.

flight attendant (n) Cabin crew on an aircraft - see also air host/hostess.

flight deck (n) Room or cabin at the front of an aircraft where the pilot and crew control the aircraft. See also cockpit.

flight number (n) Official number given to a commercial flight. All flights travelling either north or east have even flight numbers; those travelling south or west have odd numbers. e.g. The flight London to New York is 001; from New York to London it is 002.

flight plan (n) Detailed form completed by aircraft captain before flight takes off, with information about the course, duration etc. of the intended flight.

flight path (n) Course or direction of an aircraft through the air.

flipchart (n) Large sheets of paper fixed to a stand used to present information to an audience.

float (n) Money of small value notes and coins provided to to someone before they start selling things so that they can give change.

floor (n) Level in hotel or building. In Europe at ground level is the ground floor and above that the first, second, etc. In US English the floor at ground level is the first floor.

floor plan (n) Map of the inside of a building being used as an exhibition, conference area etc. showing where each stand is and also the location of other facilities.

floor show (n) Entertainment, a performance or an act in a bar or night club i.e. dancers or singers.

flotilla sailing (n) Sailing holiday where holiday-makers sail and sleep on a group of yachts.

flow chart (n) Plan or timetable showing what tasks need to be done and in what order before completing an assignment or job.

FLT. (abbr.) Flight.

fly cruise (n) Holiday-makers fly to a sea port and join a cruise ship there.

fly-drive (n) Holiday which includes flying to a destination and car hire on arrival.

flyer (n) Single sheet leaflet used for advertising.

F.O.B. (abbr.) Free On Board. Cargo which is carried free.

F.O.C. (abbr.) Free Of Charge.

foehn/föhn (n) A dry warm wind that occurs in Austria.

fog (n) Thick cloud of very small drops of water, or water vapour, in the air, which is difficult to see through.

food and beverage manager (n) Person in charge of food and drinks in a hotel, ship or conference venue, responsible for staff, finance and maintenance as well as supervising the serving of food and drink.

food court (n) Area where a number of different food outlets provide and sell food.

food poisoning (n) Illness caused by eating food that contains harmful bacteria or chemicals.

footrest (n) Small bar or support usually underneath seat in front, for passengers to rest their feet on. Found on aircraft, coaches etc.

forced landing (n) Emergency landing by an aircraft.

formalities (n) Official rules or procedures - i.e.. to show your boarding pass and passport when boarding an aircraft.

forwarding address (n) New address given when leaving accommodation to which letters and correspondance should be sent to.

foreign (adj.) Relating to or coming from a country that is not one's own.

forest (n) Large area of land covered with trees.

fossil (n) Hardened remains of a plant or an animal found inside rock.

four poster bed (n) Bed with four posts at the corners which hold up a canopy .

foyer (n) Hall or lobby of a hotel or venue.

Franc (n) Unit of currency - In France, Belgium etc.

franchise (n) Authority given by a company or organization to someone allowing them to sell its goods or services or run a business to do the same.

free house (n) Pub (Public house) that sells beers from several breweries and is not owned by one brewery (UK).

freebie (n) Journey, entrance, service or goods provided at no cost (Slang).

free port (n) Part of a port, where duties or taxes are not paid, often because the goods will be re-exported.

freeway (n) Multi-lane road (US).

frequency (n) The number of times a service occurs in a certain period - i.e. train timetables tell you of the frequency of services.

frequent flyer (n) Those who travel frequently with an airline and are sometimes rewarded with gifts or vouchers as an incentive.

fringe meeting (n) Gathering at a conference for delegates to discuss subjects not directly related to the subject of the main conferance.

frisk (n) To search a person by hand to find out if they have concealed weapons, drugs or other illegal items.

front office (n) Office responsible for the administration of a hotel reception.

front of house (n) Reception area of a hotel.

frontier (n) The area or border between one country and another country.

F.T.O. (abbr.) Federation of Tour Operators.

full **1** (n) A ticket of the maximum or adult price. **2** (adj.) complete, or with nothing available.

full board/pension (n) Accommodation that includes three meals a day.

function (n) Formal ceremony or meal.

function sheet (n) List giving details of events or functions to be held at a venue.

fuselage (n) See body.

Gg - Golf

gala dinner (n) Principal social event, especially at conference or end of a luxury tour.

Galileo (n) CRS for airlines including BA, Alitalia, Swissair, Olympic & KLM.

gale (n) Wind speed above 100 kph.

gallery (n) **1** Place where art is on display. **2** Indoor balcony in large room or theatre.

galley (n) Kitchen on boat, ship or aircraft.

game reserve (n) Conservation reserve where visitors can see wild animals in their natural habitat.

gangway (n) **1** Passageway between rows of seats. **2** Movable platform or bridge, placed between a ship and the shore, allowing people to emark and disembark.

gate (n) Exit in an airport departure lounge that leads to the aircraft.

gateway (n) **1** Main airport or port of entry to country. **2** City which forms the entrance of a geographical area.

G.B.C.O. (abbr.) Guild of British Coach Operators.

G.B.P. (abbr.) Great Britain Pound.

G.B.T.A. (abbr.) Guild of Business Travel Agents.

general sales agent (n) Agent appointed by company to act as principal or sole agent to sell services, tickets or accommodation.

geyser (n) Natural hot water spout or spring that sends water up from the ground.

G.F.I. (abbr.) Green Flag International. Association encouraging ecological awareness amongst tour operators.

gîte (n) Self-catering cottage (Fr).

glacier (n) A mass of ice, which moves, extremely slowly, sometimes through a mountain valley.

glen (n) A narrow, steep-sided valley in Scotland (UK).

gluwein (n) Spicy hot red wine drink popular in the European Alps.

G.M.T. (abbr.) Greenwich Mean Time. Usually shown by 'Z' written after the time.

gondola (n) **1** A narrow boat with a flat bottom that is particularly used in Venice as a method of transport. **2** A small cable car. See cable car.

gods (n) Gallery seats in highest part of theatre.

gorge (n) A deep and narrow valley, or opening in the earth, usually containing a river.

goodies bag (n) Amenity Kit.

G.P.C.A. (abbr.) Guild of Professional Cruise Agents.

G.P.S. (abbr.) Global Positioning System. System which helps aircraft and ships find their current location.

G.P.W.S. (abbr.) Ground Proximity Warning System.

gratis (adj.) Free.

grats. (abbr.) Gratuities.

gratuity (n) Tip, extra payment for a service.

green belt (n) An area of land around a large town or city where new developement is strictly controlled.

green card (n) **1** Insurance certificate needed by drivers of cars, when travelling out of their home country. **2** Work permit for foreign nationals in U.S.

Green Globe (n) Worldwide environmental management and awareness programme for the Travel & Tourism Industry, open to companies of any size, type and location, committed to improvements in environmental practice.

grid reference (n) To find places easily on a map, it is split into squares and divided by lines which are numbered and lettered. To locate any point on the map a note is made where these lines intersect or crossover.

grockle (n) Slang word for tourist, originated from the county of Cornwall (UK).

ground handler (n) 1Company that supplies services at a destination on behalf of a tour operator - i.e. meet and greet, check-ins, sightseeing etc. **2** Company that suplies passenger handling services on behalf on an airline.

ground services (n) Division of an airline that handles all the activities of an airline at an airport.

group (n) Collection of people, passengers or clients.

grand circle (n) Theatre seats on the first floor - usually with the best view.

G.S. (abbr.) General Sales agent.

G.S.A. (abbr.) General Sales Agent.

guard (n) **1** Official in charge of passengers on a train. **2** Official steward in a museum.

guest (n) Client, visitor or someone staying in hotel or similar accomodation.

guest house (n) Small establishment, often run by a family, that provides rented accomodation.

guest services (n) Facilities provided for the enjoyment of clients i.e. gym, restaurants, bars, library, etc.

guest services manager (n) Person in charge of seeing that clients enjoy their stay at a hotel or resort. e.g. by organising excursions, sports and introducing guests to facilities and to each other.

guide (n) Person who leads a visit or tour. A guide shows and explains local history, geography and life of a region, city or town.

guide book (n) Book, designed for tourists, giving details of history, architecture and general features of an area, town, city or country.

guided tour (n) Tour or visit led by a guide.

Guild of Sommeliers (n) International association, to which many of the top wine waiters are members.

Guilder (n) Dutch unit of currency.

gulf (n) A large inlet from the sea.

Gulf States (n) Countries in the Middle East situated around the Persian Gulf.

Hh - Hotel

half board (adj.) Accommodation including only breakfast and one main meal, normally the evening meal.

half day (adj.) Tour or event taking half a day to complete.

hall porter (n) Member of hotel staff in charge of luggage, messages, information etc. Also known as a concierge.

hamlet (n) A very small village or settlement, often without church or shops.

handicapped (adj.) Person who has a phsical or mental disability.

hand luggage (n) Luggage or baggage carried by passengers onto a coach or an aircraft.

hand outs (n) Forms, leaflets, information sheets etc. which are given out free to visitors, telling them more about a service, site, building or company.

handling fee (n) Amount charged by agent for local arrangements.

harbour (n) A small and normally well sheltered sea port.

hard currency (n) National currency which is stable and unlikely to suddenly lose its value against the currencies of other countries.

hatch (n) An opening or a door in the deck of ship or in the body of an aircraft.

H.A.T.T.A (abbr.) Hellenic (Greek) Association of Travel and Tourist Agencies.

haul (n) Part or leg of a journey i.e. Short Haul = short distance; long haul = long distance.

hazard (n) Anything that is a risk or danger.

H.C.I.M.A. (abbr.) Hotel Catering and Institutional Management Association.

headland (n) High narrow section of land that points out into the sea.

headrest cover (n) Cover, usually washable cloth, which protects the top of a seat from dirt.

head wind (n) Wind blowing from infront of an aircraft, boat or other vehicle pushing it backwards and making it travel more slowly.

health club (n) Area in a hotel or apartments that contains fitness equipment, gym and usually a swimming pool.

heatstroke (n) See sunstoke.

hectare (n) Metric measurement of land area 10,000 square metres. 1 Hectare = approx. 2.5 acres.

helicopter (n) Type of aircraft with an engine that powers overhead revolving blades (rotors) to give lift and flying capability.

helipad (n) Landing space for helicopters.

heliport (n) Airport only for helicopters.

help yourself (adj.) Self-service.

heritage (n) Relics of a country's past or history, handed down from one generation to the next.

H.H.A. (abbr.) Historic Houses Association.

high season The time of year when most people take holidays, this usually coincides with the summer months.

high tide (n) The time of the day when the sea is closest to the coast or land - See tide.

hijack (v) To take control illegally of an aircraft or other form of transport.

hiker (n) Person who travels by walking.

hill fort (n) Fortified site on top of a natural hill.

hire (v) Rent or charter.

hitch hike (v) Travel by getting free rides in other peoples' vehicles. If a coach picks up a hitch-hiker it will usually invalidate any insurance that the coach has.

hold (n) Place on an aircraft or ship where luggage is stored while in transit.

holding (n) When aircraft have to wait in the air for landing clearance when approaching an airport.

holiday (n) Time during which people relax or enjoy themselves while away from work. This may include travelling for pleasure or other leisure time activities. Vacation.

holiday camp (n) Place that provides accomodation and entertainment for large numbers of people (UK).

holiday maker (n) Person who is on holiday, usually away from home.

home exchange (n) Home owners who swap their home with others for a holiday. People wishing to do this can join an agency for a fee. They then receive a list of others who want to do the same and it is up to them to contact these home owners and exchange occupancy of their homes for their holidays.

honeymoon (n) Holiday taken by a couple after they are married.

honeypot (adj.) Well-known destination or venue that is generally over-crowded during high season.

horizon (n) The line that is seen from far distances when the sky seems to meet the sea or land.

hors d'oeuvre (n) See starter.

hospitality desk (n) An information desk usually for a particular group's use.

hospitality room (n) Room set aside for a particular group.

host (n) Man who looks after passengers or delegates.

hostess (n) Woman who looks after passengers or delegates.

hostel (n) Inexpensive hotel accommodation.

hot air balloon (n) Large balloon filled with heated air causing it to float through the air. A basket hangs from the balloon for people to travel in.

hot connection (n) When minimum connecting time for transit passengers is inside time allowed.

hotel (n) Accommodation where people pay to stay.

hotel garni (n) Hotel that provides a limited catering service to guests.

hotel manager (n) Senior management job in a hotel, responsible the running and financial success.

hotel register (n) Official record of hotel guests.

hotel voucher (n) Ticket or document used to confirm that a client has pre-paid for a hotel room.

house guide (n) Person working in a stately home, house etc. who conducts tours around the property.

housekeeper (n) Person in charge of bedrooms in a hotel.

hovercraft (n) Transport that is similar to a boat that rides on cushion of air. It can travel on land as well as water - invented by Sir Christopher Cockerill.

hub (n) Base or home port for an airline, into which it flies from other airports and passengers connect with other aircraft of the airline and fly to further destinations.

hub and spoke (n) Feeder services from small airports that are linked to services flying to other destinations.

hull (n) The main body of a boat, ship, yacht, cruise liner.

human resources department (n) Personnel department.

humid (adj.) Climate which is hot and damp. Generally very uncomfortable.

hurricane (n) An violent wind or storm. With wind speeds over 140 k.p.h.

hydro-electricity (n) Energy produced by taking power from mountain streams or rivers and rivers by damming their output.

hydrofoil (n) Boat that rides up on skis when travelling at speed.

Ii - India

I.A.C.V.B. (abbr.) International Association of Convention and Visitors' Bureaux.

I.A.P.C.O. (abbr.) International Association of Professional Congress Organisers.

I.A.T.A. (abbr.) International Air Transport Association.

I.A.T.M. (abbr.) International Association Tour Managers.

I.C.A.O. (abbr.) International Civil Aviation Organisation. Governing body for safety, communication etc.

I.C.C.A. (abbr.) International Congress and Convention Association.

iceberg (n) A large mass of ice that floats in the sea. Can be dangerous to shipping if collisions occur.

I.C.O. (abbr.) Independent Conference Organiser.

i.d. card/pass (n) Official identification pass e.g. pass used to enter security zone.

identikit destination (n) Tourist resort that copies the features of a destination that already attracts large numbers of tourists.

I.F.A.L.P.A. (abbr.) International Federation of Air Line Pilots' Associations.

I.F.E. (abbr.) Inflight Entertainment.

I.L.S. (abbr.) Instrument Landing System - used at night or in bad weather.

I.F.T.O. (abbr.) Internatinal Federation of Tour Operators.

I.F.W.T.O. (abbr.) International Federation of Women's Travel Organisations.

I.H.E.I. (abbr.) International Hotels Environment Initiative.

immigration (n) Official point on arrival in a country where identification and entry visas of passengers are checked.

immunisation (n) Vaccination against disease. See also vaccination.

impact (n) Collision or crash.

implant (n) When a travel agency puts a member of their own staff in a client company to handle bookings etc. - usually because the client company does a large amount of business with the travel agent.

inaugural flight (n) First flight on an airway route or the first flight of a new aircraft.

inbound (n) Transport or passengers coming into a country or area.

INCAD. (abbr.) Incapacitated Passenger Handling Document. Form used when a passenger needs a wheelchair.

incentive (n) Prize or award offered to encourage business or to motivate staff.

incentive travel (n) Specialised section of the industry that handles incentive travel trips.

inclusive (adj.) Items that are included in a set price or cost - i.e. accomodation with meals.

inclusive cost (n) One-off payment with no extra charges or fees added at a later time.

inclusive holiday/tour (n) Holiday package with everything included in the price.

incoming (n) Transport or passengers arriving in a country or area.

induction (n) Introductory talk to new employees, visitors etc.

induction loop (n) Closed circuit wire within a building which relays sound to a hearing aid or a simultaneous translation receiver.

industrial revolution (n) Introduction of mechanical methods of producing goods and also of large scale factories. This happened in the UK at the end of the 18th and beginning of the 19th centuries.

infant (n) Child under two years old.

inflation (n) General rise in the cost of goods and services within a country causing money to decrease in real value. When this happens it can mean that country's currency is devalued against other currencies.

in flight (n) Taking place during a journey by air.

in-flight entertainment (n) Anything offered by an airline to keep passengers entertained during a journey by air i.e. films, videos, tapes, gambling etc.

information (n) Facts or knowledge.

information board (n) Notice board used by Representatives to display notices about excursions, departure times and other resort information.

infrastructure (n) The basic necessities needed to operate a town or resort, i.e. sewage, lighting, water supply, roads and transport.

inhabitant (n) Person living in an area, town, city or country.

in-house (n) Services organised within hotel or company i.e. in-house catering at a conferance venue.

inn (n) Small pub or hotel.

inoculation (n) See vaccination.

inside cabin (n) Room on ship without a porthole or window.

insurance (n) contract whereby the insurer guarantees that a certain sum will be paid for a specified loss, injury or accident.

interaction (n) When people come to-gether and react to each other. This is often encouraged at special sessions at conferences, when people work together in small groups to produce a reaction that will bring out new ideas.

interline (n) Connections between different airlines.

interlining (n) When passengers make a journey transferring between different airlines while using only one ticket.

international driving permit/licence (n) Permit carried by car drivers that enables them to drive in a country outside their own.

international date line (n) An imaginary line that approximately follows 180° longitude. Travellers moving east to west over this line gain an extra day. Those moving from west to east lose a day.

international money order (n) Bank draft drawn in the currency of the receiving country. e.g. a US dollar invoice can be paid with a dollar money order drawn on a UK bank.

Interpol (n) International Police agency.

interpreter (n) Person who translates verbally from one language to another.

interpretation centre (n) Office or facility giving an explanation of a site of interest, nature reserve, etc.

in transit (adj.) 1 People or goods that are currently travelling. 2 When passengers lay over or stay in a country that is not their final destination usually without leaving airside or customs area of an airport.

invisible exports (n) Income recieved by a country from trading in services rather than goods. Invisible exports include tourism, banking, shipping and investments. Goods are counted as visible exports.

invitation (n) Request to attend a function.

invoice (n) List of goods or services supplied, including their prices. See also bill.

I.O.J. (abbr.) Institute Of Journalists .

I.O.L. (abbr.) Institute Of Linguists.

Iron Age (n) Historical period after the Bronze Age when iron started to be used to make tools and weapons. Approximately 500 BC.

irrigation (n) Method of supplying water to land or crops by means of small channels or pipes.

island (n) Area of land completely surrounded by water.

isthmus (n) A narrow strip of land surrounded by sea, connecting two larger areas of land.

itinerary (n) Detailed description, record or plan of a visit, tour, journey or route.

I.T. (abbr.) **1** Inclusive Tour. **2** Information Technology.

I.T.A.A. Irish Travel Agents Association.

I.T.C. (abbr.) Inclusive Tours by Charter.

I.T.M.A. (abbr.) Incentive Travel and Meetings Association.

I.T.T. (abbr.) Institute of Travel and Tourism.

I.T.X. (abbr.) Inclusive Tour excursions - usually applied to an air fare.

Jj - Juliet

J.A.A. (abbr.) Joint Aviation Authority.

J.A.L. (abbr.) Japan Airlines.

Jacuzzi (n) Large warm bath with jets of water - often communal.

jet (n) Aircraft propelled by jet engines.

jetfoil (n) Fast boat that rides up on skis while at speed. A hydrofoil is similar.

jet lag (n) A feeling of tiredness and confusion after a long journey by air, normally when passengers travel between time zones.

jetliner (n) Airliner (US).

jet stream (n) Strong wind that blows in the atmosphere several miles above the Earth.

jetty (n) **1** Small pier projecting into water. **2** Airbridge - Movable corridor brought to the doors of an aircraft to allow people to exit and to enter from the airport.

joining instructions (n) Letter sent to passengers or delegates confirming details of travel arrangements including times and dates.

journey (n) Travelling from one place to another.

jumbo jet (n) Boeing 747 (slang).

jump seat (n) Crew seat in an aircraft that retracts (jumps) back against a bulkhead.

Kk - Kilo

keep (n) Area of a castle, usually a tower in the middle of the castle, that was easy to guard and defend, where the food and stores were kept in the event of a siege.

key card (n) Small plastic card with a magnetic strip, similar to a credit card, used for security reasons instead of keys for hotel rooms and ships' cabins

keynote speech (n) Important speech setting the theme of a meeting or conference.

kiddies representative (n) See nanny. Usually associated with the less wealthy parents.

kilometre (n) Metric unit of distance. One kilometre = 1,000 metres or 0.62 miles.

king size bed (n) Large double bed.

kiosk (n) **1** Small box-like structure from which tickets, programmes etc. can be purchased. **2** Small shop or concession selling newspapers, cigarettes etc. See concession and box office.

kitchen porter (n) The most junior position/job in a kitchen, involving washing-up and vegetable preparation. Also known as a plongeur.

K.L.M. (abbr.) Koninkiij Luchvaart Maatschappij. Dutch national airline. The oldest airline in the world still operating under the original name.

knee biters (n) Slang used in museums and tourist venues to describe children.

knock on effect (n) When an initial action or event causes several other actions or events to happen. i.e. If oil prices increase, it has has a knock-on effect on transport costs and therefore holiday pricing.

knot (n) Nautical measurement of one nautical mile per hour.

K.P.H. (abbr.) Kilometres Per Hour.

Ll - Lima

L.A.I. (abbr.) Local Area Initiative - partnership set up between the Tourist Boards, Local Authorities, other agencies and private firms with clearly defined objectives. Programmes agreed between partners usually run for a three year term.

land **1** (n) An area of ground. **2** (v) When an aircraft or ship arrives after a journey.

landfall (n) The first sight of land after a voyage by sea.

landing card (n) Form filled in by passengers and handed to the immigration on arrival in a country.

landmark (n) A particular physical feature that can be easily noticed by travellers, in order to judge their position.

landscape (n) Geographical area that has a distinctive appearance when looking across it. It can be natural or man-made.

landscape architect (n) Designer of gardens, parks and plants and trees. Probably the most famous was Capability' Brown, who re-designed the park lands surrounding stately homes such as Blenheim Palace and Stowe School. He was known as 'Capability' because of his frequent comments that an area had capabilities.

langlauf (n) Cross country skiing particularly popular in Scandinavia . Also known as Nordic skiing.

lapel mike (n) Small microphone that can be clipped onto a person's clothes.

L.A.T.A. (abbr.) Latin American Travel Association.

late bookings (n) Bookings made at the last time possible, sometimes incurring extra charges.

Latin America (n) Central and South America.

latitude (n) Distance measured in degrees, north or south from the equator.

layover (n) **1** Compulsory stop, usually overnight, for aircrew who otherwise would be working more than their permitted hours. **2** Where passengers break a journey due to lack of connecting flights.

L.C.O. (abbr.) Lowest Cost Operator.

leakage (n) Any factor which causes profits from tourism to be taken away from the place where the tourism occurs.

lease (v) Rent or hire - usually applied to capital items such as aircraft, cars boats or property.

lectern (n) Stand with angled top on which a speaker or lecturer can put their script or reference material and read from it while speaking to an audience.

leg (n) Section of a journey.

leisure activity (n) Sport or recreational activity that is carried out in the time that a person is away time away from work.

leisure card (n) Card given by some UK local authorities to local rate payers, entitling them to free or reduced price use of leisure amenities/facilities.

leisure day visitor (n) Someone who visits an attraction or venue such as a Theme park or stately home for one day.

leisure industry (n) Companies providing the means, facilities and equipment for people to utilise their leisure time.

leisure time (n) Time away from work or other duties in which recreational activities etc. can be done.

Le Shuttle (n) Trade name for the channel tunnel car and passenger carrying train service between the UK and France.

lessee (n) Client that rents space in a building or in a conference venue.

lessor (n) Official working on behalf of the owners of a building or a conferance venue that rents out space or facilities.

let down (v) When the wheels or undercarriage of an aircraft are lowered into position, ready for landing.

L.H.R. (abbr.) London Heathrow Airport.

liable (adj.) When a company has a legal responsibility for something.

liability (n) The maximum amount (money) for which a company or organisation is liable for something.

licence (n) Formal or legal permission to operate something, carry out a service or drive a vehicle.

licensed (n) Bar or place which can serve alcohol.

licensee (n) The person to whom the authorities have granted permission to sell alcohol on specified premises.

life belt (n) A large bouyant/floating ring used to keep a person afloat in the sea in an emergency.

life boat (n) **1** Small boat carried by a ship which people can use to escape if there is any danger of the ship sinking or in the event of an emergency. **2** Rescue boat sent out help people if they are in danger at sea.

lifeguard (n) A person who works at a swimming pool or a section of beach, who rescues people when they are in danger of drowning.

life jacket (n) Inflatable or bouyant clothing which keeps a person afloat in water. Life vest or life preserver.

life raft (n) Inflatable boat or floating flat structure used at sea in the event of an emergency. Found on an aircraft or a ship.

life preserver (n) See life jacket.

life vest (n) See life jacket.

lifeboat drill (n) An exercise or activity on a ship to familarise the passengers with what they would have to do in an emergency, should they need to abandon ship.

lift (n) Mechanical platform which travels between floors within a building (UK). Elevator (US).

light aircraft (n) Small aeroplane that can only carry a few passengers.

lilo (n) Inflatable rubber or plastic bed that is used by holiday makers to float on the sea or lie on while sunbathing.

limousine (n) Large car with a driver.

liner (n) Large passenger ship, often used for cruises.

linkman (n) Doorman who stands outside a luxury hotel.

Lira (n) Italian unit of currency.

listed building (n) Building of historical merit protected legally, so that it cannot be demolished or altered without the permission of the local authotrity (UK).

liqueur (n) Strong alcohol based drink, usually drunk at the end of a meal.

load factor (n) Percentage occupancy of seats on transport.

L.O. (abbr.) Last Orders e.g. for meals or drinks.

lobby (n) Reception area in a hotel.

local time (n) The official time in a region or a country.

location (n) Position where something or someone in situated or positioned.

locator (n) Computer booking reference, given by airlines and tour operators.

loch (n) Scottish or Irish lake, or inlet of the sea.

logo (n) Symbol or design, used by an organisation or a company as its sign.

long haul (n) Long distance flight, usually over 6 hours flying time.

longitude (n) Angular distance east or west on the earth's surface, measured in degrees from the prime meridian, 0°, which passes through Greenwich in London, England.

loss leader (adj.) Low price product or service, that does not make a profit, offered as an incentice to attract more customers to a company so that they will purchase profitable items in the future.

lost property (n) Personal possessions that have been lost, stolen or mislaid.

lost property office (n) Room where lost items are stored when they are found.

lough (n) See loch.

lounge (n) Seating area. Usually where people wait, such as in a hotel or departure lounge at an airport.

low season (adj.)The time of year when people do not usually go holiday, this usually coincides with the winter. Off season.

low tide (n) The time of the day when the sea is furthest from the coast or land - See tide.

luggage (n) Personal possessions packed in bags or cases for travelling. Baggage.

lunch (n) Meal served in the middle of the day.

Mm - Mike

mailing list (n) A list of names and addresses of people or organisations to which advertising or promotional material is sent.

mailshot (n) Advertising sent by post.

maitre d'hotel (n) Person in charge of the service in a restaurant.

manager (n) Person in charge, the most senior administrator.

manifest (n) List of passengers or cargo.

manual ticket issue (n) Issuing tickets for transport by hand, instead of by computer.

mansard (n) Windows that look like 'eyes' at top of 17th century French buildings.

manual (n) Book of instructions and or company rules.

map (n) A drawing or representation of an area of land, a city or a country, designed to represent locations in relation to each other, usually with a grid of lines across it, so particular locations can be found easily by noting where the lines of the grid intersect (grid reference).

M.A.P. (abbr.) Modified American Plan. Hotel accommodation including breakfast and one main meal.

maquis (n) Area of open uncultivated land found in southern France.

marina (n) Man-made harbour for boats and yachts, usually with long term berths for small boats.

Mark (n) German unit of currency.

mark-up (n) The differnce between the cost of a product and the amount at which it is sold.

marker (n) **1** Tall tour group member appointed by the tour guide, so the group can see this person in a crowd, this helps to keep the group together.

market (n) **1** An area where traders set up stalls to sell goods. **2** The amount of people who want, or who are able to buy a product.

marketing (n) The planning and action of promoting and selling a product.

market research (n) Study of needs or requirements of customers to find out how and why they buy goods or services.

market share (n) Proportion of the total sales of a particular product or sevice gained by a particular company.

marquee (n) Large tent, usually hired for special occasions.

mast (n) Tall upright pole that support the sails on a boat/yacht.

master key (n) Hotel key that can unlock all of the rooms in the hotel and is used by hotel staff to gain access to rooms for cleaning etc.

mayday mayday (adj.) International radio distress call.

matinee (n) Afternoon performance in a theatre or cinema.

M.B.O. (abbr.) **1** Maintenance and Buildings Officer - British ski companies' term that has been adopted to mean Muscle Bound Oaf in slang.

M.C.O. (abbr.) Miscellaneous Charges Order. Airline voucher used to cover collection of funds.

M.C.T. (abbr.) Minimum Connect Time.

meander (n) **1** Large bend in a river. **2** A road, river, trail etc. which has a lot of bends along its course. **3** To walk somewhere in a leisurely or aimless way.

medical kit (n) Pack that contains the basics needed to deal with minor accidents. By law, in most countries, coaches, planes and other forms of public transport have to carry a medical kit.

Mediterranean (n) Sea between Europe and Africa. Also used to describe the areas of southern europe that border the Mediterranean sea.

meet and greet (n) A service welcoming visitors as they arrive at a port of entry.

meeting (n) When a group of people come together for discussion.

megalith (n) A large stone that was sited by people, possibly as a monument, between 3000 - 2000 BC. i.e. Stonehenge is a collection of megaliths arranged in a circle.

M.E.L. (abbr.) Minimum Equipment List (aircraft).

menu (n) List, usually listing different types of food available.

meridian (n) A line on a map passing through the North Pole and the South Pole.

metro (n) Underground system, particularly associated with Paris. See underground.

M.I.A. (abbr.) Meetings Industry Association.

Michelin (n) French Tyre manufacturer who publish maps and guide books. These products where originally designed to encourage travellers to drive cars, and, therefore, use Michelin tyres. Michelin developed a series of maps to make it easier for drivers to go from place to place. Also published are restaurant and hotel guides, and country/ area guides, all to encourage car travel.

Michelin Star (n) Michelin guides grade the best restaurants and give them

from one to three stars based on their general standard. Three stars being the maximum and representing the highest standard.

microphone (n) Device which turns sound into electrical signals. Usually used to make sound louder (amplify it via speakers), or to record it (with audio recording equipment).

Middle East (n) Countries bordering Eastern Mediterranean and the Persian Gulf including Bahrain, Egypt, Iran, Iraq, Israel, Jordan, Kuwait, Lebanon, Oman, Palestine, Qatar, Saudi Arabia, United Arab Emirates and Yemen.

midnight sun (n) Found within the Arctic Circle when there are nights without darkness. This occurs in midsummer when the sun can often be seen shining at midnight. Many visitors make special trips to northern Scandinavia during mid-June to see this phenomena.

midweek (n) Usually refers to Tuesday, Wednesday and Thursday - i.e. a midweek holiday does not include the weekend.

mike (n) Microphone.

milk run (n) Tour that is easy to sell tickets for, because it follows the most popular, and generally overcrowded, routes.

minibar (n) Small refrigerator in hotel bedrooms or ship cabins, stocked with drinks, snacks etc.

minibreak (n) A short holiday away from home.

minimum stay (n) The shortest time before traveller can use the return section of a ticket, without paying a higher fare. i.e. a return ticket from London to Paris costs less if you stay in Paris for a minmum of three nights.

minutes (n) **1** Division of time, 60 minutes = 1 hour. **2** Formal written record of a meeting. **3** A devision of degrees on a map, 1 degree (1°) = 60 minutes (60').

mirage (n) Illusion created by hot air bending light rays, usually distortions that look like water, but, sometimes other objects can be reflected and become visible.

mishandled luggage (n) Luggage damaged while in transit with an airline.

misrouted luggage (n) Luggage that has been misplaced or sent to the wrong destination by an airline.

mobile (adj.) Portable or moveable.

moderator (n) Person who is in charge of discussions at a conference or meeting.

modular (n) **1** Exhibition stands that are of standard sizes and are used at many different exhibitions. **2** Courses that use the same lectures and material in units or modules. Each unit can be taught individually, without direct reference to other units.

mogul (n) Large hump on a ski slope.

money back (n) Return of sum of money paid for a particular product or service, especially if it is not satisfactory or faulty.

monsoon (n) **1** Wind that blows across the Indian Ocean which blows from the north west in the winter and the south west in the summer. **2** Wet weather season during the summer in regions of Southern Asia and the Far East that comes with the summer monsoon.

moor (n) **1** Open uncultivated land (UK). **2** To attach a boat or ship to land or a fixed point.

mosaic (n) Picture or design made by inlaying small pieces of coloured glass or stone in mortar.

motel (n) Hotel catering for car travellers, which provides parking space near to the rooms.

mothers' room (n) See parents' room.

M.P.H. (abbr.) miles per hour - a measurement of speed of a car, train, lorry etc.

M.P.P.A. (abbr.) Million Passengers Per Annum.

M.T.A.A. (abbr.) Multiple Travel Agents Association.

mule (n) Person used by a smuggler to carry illegal substances or goods on their behalf.

multilateral (n) Agreement between three or more countries.

multi-screen projection (n) Different images projected onto different screens at the same time.

multi-sector (adj.) Several sectors or portions - i.e. a company that works in more than one sector of the travel industry by providing hotel accommodation and travel.

museum (n) Building or venue housing items of historical, scientific and/or local importance.

Nn - November

N/A (abbr.) Not Applicable or Not Available.

N.A.H.C. (abbr.) National Association of Holiday Centres.

NAITA (acr.) National Association of Independent Travel Agents.

nanny (n) A woman who is paid by parents to look after their child or children. A nanny is usually employed by wealthier people and is associated with more expensive holidays.

narrow boat (n) Boats used on canals, often hired out for holidays (UK).

national park (n) A large area of land which has been taken over and protected by Government or national authority because of its natural beauty. Probably the first National Park was Yellowstone, designated a National Park by US Congress in 1872. British National Parks were started in 1949 by the National Parks and Access to the Countryside Act.

nationality (n) To have been born in a particular country, therefore, have a legal right to be citizen and to be able to live in the country.

native (n) 1. Belonging to a particular country i.e. being born/bought up in a particular country 2. (adj) To be of a particular country.

nautical mile (n) Measurement of distance by sea or air. 1 nautical mile = approx. 1.85km or 1.15 miles.

N.E.A. (abbr.) National Exhibitors Association.

necessities bag (n) Given to airline passengers who have lost their luggage, it contains basic necessities such as washing kit etc.

neck mike (n) Microphone worn on a chain around the neck.

negative (adj.) No.

Neoplan (n) German coach manufacturing company well known for making double-deck coaches.

next of kin (n) A person's closest living relatives or family.

niche marketing (n) Marketing directed to a particular section of the market that has its own special needs or interests. e.g. particular age groups.

night club (n) Place of entertainment open at night. Usually serves alcoholic drinks, sometimes food and has facilities for dancing.

night manager (n) Senior member of staff in charge of hotel at night.

night porter (n) Often only porter on duty at night, duties may include supervising the reception desk, the check-in of late arrivals, and supplying food if the hotel offers 24 hour room service.

night sheets (n) Covers used to protect an exhibition stand at night, while the exhibition is closed.

N.N.E.B. (abbr.) Nursery Nurse Examination Board. A qualification that is often needed to work supervising children for a tour operator.

N.T. (abbr.) National Trust. Charitable organisation that preserves houses and countryside (UK).

N.O.E.A. (abbr.) National Outdoor Events Association.

nomad (n) Member of tribe that moves from area to area with no permanent living place.

noon (n) Midday, 12:00pm.

Nordic (n) Of, or from Scandinavian

countries (Northern Europe).

northern lights (n) Aurora Borealis.

North Pole (n) The most northern point of the world.

no show (adj.) Guest, delegate or passenger with a reservation who does not claim their reserved place.

nose (n) Front end of an aircraft.

notice (n) Announcement, bulletin or sign giving instructions.

nozzle (n) Outlet or pipe delivering cooled air or liquid.

N.T.O. (abbr.) National Tourist Office/ Organisation.

N.V.Q. (abbr.) National Vocational Qualification.

Oo - Oscar

O.A.G. (abbr.) Official Airlines Guide.

O.& D. (abbr.) Origin and Destination.

oasis (n) A fertile place in a desert which has a natural water supply.

O.A.P. (abbr.) Old Age Pensioner.

observatiion area (n) An area at an airport where aircraft enthusiasts can watch the aircraft. It is also used by people watching their friends and relatives departing.

obstruct (v) To be in the way of or to block the passage of somebody or something.

ocean (n) The major seas that cover 70% of the world's surface.

oceanarium (n) Display of sea animals that is open to the public.

oceanography (n) Scientific study of the oceans.

occupancy (n) The amount of people using a facility or venue.

occupancy rate (n) Percentage of clients that have seats, hotel rooms, cruise cabins etc. on a particular journey

off duty (adj.) When someone is officially not working.

off peak (adj.) A period of time when demand is usually low.

off loaded (v) When people or goods are taken from, or leave transport.

off season (n) The time of year when people do not usually go on holiday - this usually coincides with the winter months.

officer (n) 1 Official representative of a structured organisation. 2 Senior crew member usually in charge of passengers and crew on a ship or an aircraft etc.

O.F.T. (abbr.) Office of Fair Trading.

O.H.P. (abbr.) Over Head Projector.

O.K. (adj.) When written on an airline ticket it means return flight does not have to be re-confirmed, or has already been re-confirmed.

onboard (adj.) To be situated in or on transport.

on foot (n) Walking.

on-line (n) Connections by the same airline.

on site (adj.) On the premises.

one way (n) Single outward journey.

onshore (adj) To be on land.

OPEC (acr.) Organisation of Petroleum Exporting Countries: Algeria, Gabon, Indonesia, Iran, Iraq, Kuwait, Libya, Nigeria, Qatar, Saudi Arabia, United Arab Emirates and Venezuela, which periodically fixes the price of oil. As a major portion of airline costs are for fuel, when this organisation increases prices it has has a knock-on effect on airline ticket and travel pricing.

open date (n) Return portion of ticket that can be used on any day and without an advance reservation.

open jaw (n) Airline ticket that allows stop-overs and/or different routes on the outward and inward journeys

open space concept (adj.) At meetings and conferences delegates have no set agenda.

open skies (n) Air space not regulated by any government or organisation.

operations room (n) Control room for coach operators, airlines, tour operators giving the latest travel information and co-ordinating events.

operator (n) Company offering tours and/or transport.

option (n) Choice or alternative.

optional (adj.) Left to choice whether to pay or do something.

outward (n) Departing leg of a return journey.

Ordnance Survey (n) Official map-making organisation in UK. It gets its name because the first maps were made for the army. Ordnance means artillery.

Ordnance Survey Maps (n) Very detailed large scale maps of all areas of Britain.

organic (adj.) Method of producing food crops that does not use artificial chemicals or fertilisers.

orientation tour (n) Short familiarisation tour on arrival in a town or city. Usually carried out by Courier or Tour Manager, not a local guide.

O.R.V. (abbr.) Oesterreichischer Reiseburo Verband. Austrian Travel Agent's Association.

O.S. (abbr.) Ordnance Survey.

outbound (n) People or transport going out from, or leaving an area or country.

outskirts (n) Suburbs of a town or city.

out of pocket expenses (n) Personal money paid out on behalf of a company which will be reimbursed, by the company to the person, at a later stage.

over (adj.) During radio communication 'over' signifies that information has been given and it is now the other communicators turn to talk/reply.

overbooking (n) Numbers booked exceed amount of places available.

overcharge (v) To unintentionally or intentionally charge someone too much money for goods or sevices.

overhead projector (n) Equipment which projects an image onto a screen from a large transparency.

overhead stowage lockers (n) Installed in coaches and aircraft to provide, closed containers for storing passengers hand luggage.

overlook (v) To forget or ignore something.

overnight bag (n) Bag carried as hand luggage containing basic necessities for overnight journey or one night away.

overriding commission (n) **1** Extra commission paid to a travel agent who reaches a sales target. **2** Additional money paid by a principal tour operator to an agent who is the middleman between the sales agent and the principal tour operator. The amount paid is based on the level of sales of the sales agent.

ozone (n) Form of oxygen found especially in the upper atmosphere of the Earth, which blocks some of the sun's harmful rays.

Pp - Papa

P.A. (abbr.) Public Address system.

package/package tour/package holiday (n) A holiday that is arranged by a tour operator and bought by customers, that includes accommodation, travel and food.

packed lunch **(n)** Cold meal that is prepared in advance and can be carried.

pampas (n) Grasslands and open areas of Southern America.

Paradore (n) Spanish government owned chain of hotels built in a local Spanish style and offering traditional Spanish food.

parasol (n) A large umbrella that is found on the beach or by a swimming pool that protects people from the sun's rays.

parents' room (n) A room at an airport terminal where parents' can attend to their childrens' needs such as feeding, clothes changing etc. Parents' rooms can now also be found at railway stations and other transport terminals.

parish (n) **1** An area in England that has it's own elected council. **2** A village or an area of a town that has it's own church.

park (n) A public area with grass and trees that people can go to relax. Usually found in towns and cities.

park and ride (n) Where visitors are encouraged to park their cars outside an urban area (town or city) and ride into the centre of the town/city on a bus to prevent congestion from cars in the town or city.

Pars (n) CRS for TWA and Northwest Airlines.

part charter (n) When only some of the seats on an aircraft are chartered by a tour operator(s).

partition (n) Movable interior wall.

passenger (n) A person travelling in or on transport.

passport (n) An official indentity document that is used by people to enter countries other than one's own.

passport control (n) The place at an airport/border or a port where visitors have to show their passports, when entering/leaving a country.

P.A.T.A. (abbr.) Pacific Asia Travel Association.

PAX (acr.) Passengers.

P.C.O. (abbr.) Professional Conference Organiser.

P.C.V. (abbr.) Passenger Carrying Vehicle.

peak season (n) See high season

peninsula (n) A long piece of land that is almost completely surrounded by sea that is attached to other land at one point only.

pension (n) Small European hotel, often without a restaurant.

perk/perks (n) A special benefit to someone doing a particular job. Working for an airline means that the empolyees get cheap airfares.

permit (v) **1** To allow. **2** (n) Official pass or authorisation.

personal space (n) The area around an individual which if a stranger enters the person is worried, frightened, embarrassed or annoyed. Everyone has their own definition of personal space, and some nationalities will permit closer contact than others.

Personality girl/model/staff (n) Temporary staff used to add glamour to an exhibition or conference.

peseta (n) Spanish unit of currency.

P.G. (abbr.) **Paying Gu**est - usually in a private house.

photogrammetry (n) Using photos to obtain measurements, particularly for making maps.

picnic (n) A meal eaten outdoors, usually sitting on the grass or on the beach.

pilgrim (n) Person who travels for religious reasons usually to visit a shrine, temple or ther site of religious importance.

pilot (n) **1** Crew member who flies an aircraft and is responsible for the passengers and other crew. **2** Registered official who guides large ships into a harbour or guides large ships through dangerous waters.

P.I.R. (abbr.) Property Incident Report. Used for lost luggage.

pirate (n) Someone who overcharges for a service who is also operating illegally.

piste (n) A track of firm snow for skiing on.

pitch **1** (n) Distance between the front edge of one seat and the seat behind. **2** (v) To put erect a tent.

pit stop (n) A quick stop for refreshments when on a journey.

place of origin (n) The country, town, city where someone or something has originated from.

P.L.C. (abbr.) Public Limited Company (UK).

P.L.A. (abbr.) Port of London Authority. Governing body for the River Thames (UK).

platform (n) **1** The area of a railway station where passengers embark and diembark from the train. **2** A raised stage or horizontal surface that is used by speakers or performers to enable them to be seen.

plastic (n) Credit cards or charge cards. (slang).

plat du jour (n) Dish of the day - Chef's dish of the day in a restaurant (Fr.).

plongeur (n) Person who is employed to wash up dishes etc. in a hotel or restaurant.

plonky kit (n) Pack carried by cabin crew on an aircraft with alcohol, sewing kit and essential emergency items.

ploughman's lunch (n) Meal consisting of bread, cheese and pickle - often served in country pubs (UK).

P.M. (abbr.) Afternoon or evening.

polder (n) A Dutch (Netherlands) word for land that has been reclaimed from the sea. Usually farmland

pollution (n) Usually caused by human activity discharging rubbish into public areas, noxious substances into the air or rubbish into water.that causes the production of bacteria. It can also be unacceptable levels of noise or nasty smells such as burning rubber.

pool (n) **1** Swimming pool. **2** (v) Agreement where two or more transport carriers agree to promote one route and divide the revenue obtained from the route. **3** Agreement to collect tips or revenue and divide them up equally.

population (n) The number of people that inhabit an area or country.

port (n) **1** Harbour for ships. **2** Also nautical term for the left side of a boat or ship when looking at it from the rear/back.

port charge (n) Charged by local authorities to passengers to pay for port facilities

porter (n) Person who carries luggage

at a hotel, hospital or a railway station.

porterage (n) The act of carrying luggage.

postcard (n) A thin piece of card, usually with a picture on one side, that people use to write to friends while on holiday or away from home.

pound (n) 1.The unit of currency used in UK. Also used in other countries. See countries of the world. 2. A unit of weight mainly used in UK and US.

pousada (n) Portuguese Government owned hotel built in local Portuguese style that offers Portuguese food

powder skiing (n) Off-piste ski-ing on fresh snow

powder snow (n) New snow that has just fallen.

prairies (n) Large area of grassland found in North America. Prairies have very few trees.

pre-board passengers (n) Passengers allowed onto transport in advance of other passengers i.e. disabled passengers boarding an aircraft first.

pre-arrival checks (n) Checks carried out before clients arrive, usually to confirm transport, accommodation, arrival time.

preferential (adj) Giving an advantage i.e. preferential rate.

preliminary draft (n) First version of a paper or document which is subject to further amendment

premium traffic (n) Passengers paying higher fares i.e. Passengers paying business or first class fares on airlines.

prepaid (adj) Paid in advance.

preservation (n) The protection of an historic building or an area of land.

pressurised (adj) When the air pressure in an aircraft cabin is kept as near to that of sea level as possible.

prestel (n) British Computerised Infor-mation System, generally used in Travel Agencies

prevailing wind (n) The most frequent wind direction at a location.

private facilities (n) En-suite bathroom

proforma (n) An invoice raised in advance of a booking, when a company or service provider wants payment in advance.

programme (n) Timetable of events.

projector (n) Machine that projects films and slides onto a screen.

promotion (n) Event that increases the public's awareness of goods, services, venue etc.

promotional fare (n) Fares at a specially reduced price to encourage the use of the route or the method of transport.

proprietor (n) The owner of a hotel, guest house, shop.

P.I.R (abbr.) Property Irregularity Report - completed by passengers to help them find lost luggage.

place card (n) A small card that has a person's name written on it, which is put on a table at a formal meal to indicate where that person is to sit.

plenary session (n) Session in which all delegates participate

podium (n) Raised platform on which a someone stands or sits.

post- (prefix) After e.g. Post-Conference tour = tour that takes place after a conference finishes.

pre- (prefix) Before e.g. Pre-Conference tour = tour that takes place before a conference starts.

press release (n) Leaflet/information sent to Journalists and the media (newspapers/magazines/journals), that publicises a new product or service.

pro rata (adj) Agreement to divide up revenue.

P.R.S. (abbr.) Performing Rights Society. An organisation that issues licences that enables people to play music on coaches and in a public places.

P.S.A. (abbr.) Passenger Shipping Association.

P.S.V. (abbr.) Public Service Vehicle.

P/U (abbr.) Pick-Up, i.e. to pick up passengers.

pub (n) A building that has one or more bars that sells alcoholic and non alcoholic drinks to people. (UK)

public holiday (n) Day during which all government offices and banks are closed.

public house (n) See pub.

public liability insurance (n) Insurance carried to ensure that passengers are covered in the event of an operator being accountable for a mishap or accident.

public transport (n) Transportation owned by the state (government) such as buses and trains, that is used by the public buying their own tickets.

publicity (n) Information or actions that makes a person or place better known to the public

pullman (n) A railway company or a railway carraige that offers extreme luxury to the passengers.

pullman car (n) A raiway carraige that provides beds for people to sleep in (US). See sleeping car (UK).

punctual (adj) To be on time.

punctuality (n) The act of being on time.

Punt (n) Pound. Unit of currency in Eire (Republic of Ireland).

pull (v) 1. to attract. 2. (n) An attraction. 3. (v) To cancel.

punter (n) Passenger, client or customer (slang).

purser (n) Person in charge of the welfare of the passengers on a ship or an aircraft.

Qq - Quebec

QANTAS (acr.) Queensland and Northern Territories Aerial Services. Australian National airline.

Q. & A. session (abbr.) Question and Answer session, usually at the end of a meeting, speach or discussion.

Q/C aircraft (abbr.) Quick Change aircraft. An aircraft that can easily convert between carrying passengers and/or freight.

quake. (abbr.) Earthquake.

qualification (n) Skill, experience, or examination passed, that makes a person suitable for a particular vacancy or job.

quality **1** (n) The standard of goods or services when compared with similar goods or services. **2** (adj.) Something which is of a high standard.

quality control (n) System for maintaining standards of goods and services.

QUANGO (acr.) Quasi-Autonomous Non-Governmental Organisation. A committee appointed by the government which works independently. These committees have responsibility for particular areas of activity - i.e. the giving of government grants.

quarantine (n) Period of time during which humans or animals are kept away from others to reduce the risk of disease spreading, because they may be or are infected.

quay (n) Platform next to the sea or a river where boats or ships can berth, load and unload.

queen size bed (n) Double bed.

queue (n) People or vehicles in line one behind the other that are waiting for something.

quicksand (n) Wet sand which can be dangerous, as normally it will not support the weight of a person.

quilt (n) Duvet.

quota (n) Quantity or size of official allocation.

quote (n) Price or estimate for goods or services.

Rr - Romeo

R.A.C. (abbr.) Royal Automobile Club (UK).

rack (n) Ledges above or at the ends of seats on transport, where passengers can store their luggage.

rack rate (n) Normal price for a hotel room to individual clients.

radar (n) A system of discovering the position or speed of objects such as aircraft or ships when they cannot been. This is done by the use of radio signals.

rails (n) Metal bars on which train wheels run.

railway (n) Company that provides transport by train.

Ramadan (n) Islamic religious event which takes place in the ninth month of the Muslim calendar. During Ramadam Muslims do not eat between sunrise and sunset.

ramp (n) 1 Sloping passage to make wheelchair access easier. 2 Steps leading up to an aircraft.

Rapide (n) Brand name for National Express Coaches which has host/hostess refreshment service.

rapids (n) Section of a river which is fast flowing, often shallow and rocky.

rapporteur (n) Official who is appointed to attend a conferance or meeting and write a report or a summary.

rate of exchange (n) The price at which one currency is valued compared with other currencies.

rebate (n) Refund of money after goods or services have been purchased.

re-book (v) To book or order again.

reclaimed land (n) Land that has been made usable for building or agriculture by draining or making a barrier against the sea, etc.

reclining seats (n) Seats that have an adjustable back which can be tilted backward or forward.

receipt (n) Formal written confirmation that goods or payment have been received.

reception (n) Area in a hotel, campsite, accommodation or other venue, where guests are welcomed, checked in, issued keys etc.

receptionist (n) Person who works in a reception area.

reconfirm (n) To confirm or check a booking that has already been made.

recreation (n) Activity done for pleasure in time away from work.

recycle (n) To re-use resources i.e. to re-use empty bottles.

refund (v) To pay money back after it has been spent. Rebate.

refreshments (n) Food and drink.

regatta (n) Event at which races are held between boats.

region (n) Area of land that is different from other ares of land because it has individual features.

register 1 (n) Official record of attendance or people staying in a hotel. **2** (v) To sign the official register of attendance or to check in at hotel or conference. **3** (n) Log book of a ship.

registered baggage (n) Luggage given to the carrier and not the responsibility of the passenger until claimed at end of the journey.

registration (n) Check in for conference or exhibition.

registration form (n) Form on which

delegates confirm booking for a conference, giving details of their requirements.

reimburse (v) To pay money back after it has been spent. Refund, rebate.

relay interpreter (n) One interpreter at a meeting who translates a minority language into a common language for the other interpreters to listen to and translate into their own language. e.g. a conference where a Romanian speaker is translated by relay interpreter into English and then other interpreters translate into Japanese, Arabic and German etc.

rental charges (n) Money paid for the use or hire of equipment, vehicle or a venue.

Rep. (abbr.) Representative.

repatriation (n) To be brought home to a home country e.g. Emergency repatriation insurance is taken out by travellers to ensure that when they are away from home, if they are seriously ill or injured, they can be flown home.

report (n) Official written details of events or happenings. These can be weekly reports sent to a company by their staff, complaints, transport details, weekly hotel or accommodation reports, customer services report forms, and many other sorts of written information.

representative (n) Person appointed by a company to work at a resort or tourist area looking after clients.

request (v) To ask politely for something.

research (n) Investigation or study to discover or establish facts.

residence (n) Place where someone lives.

resort (n) Area with accommodation and facilities, especially for tourists.

resort representative (n) Person who represents a company in a resort or tourist area looking after the clients of that particular company.

restaurant (n) Public place where meals can be bought and eaten.

restaurant car (n) Carriage of a train that serves food to passengers.

rest room (n) Lavatory or toilet in a public place (US).

return (n) 1 Leg of a journey that is coming back to the original point of departure. 2 Ticket that includes the outward and inward legs of a journey.

revalidate (v) 1 Officially reconfirm or re-instate. 2 Officially change ticket and to make it valid for travel.

reveal (n) When a new product is shown to a sales force for the first time at a conference.

reverse thrust (n) Push or thrust of a jet engine when it is reversed, to act as a brake and to slow down an aircraft when landing.

ridge and furrow (n) Features in a field where ploughing, since the Middle Ages, has formed a set of parallel ridges.

rip-off (v) 1 To intentionally charge someone too much money for goods and services (Slang). 2 (adj) When something has cost too much money (Slang).

riviera (n) Coastal area of natural beauty and good climate.

room service (n) Service in a hotel which provides snacks, meals and drinks and delivers them to a room.

rooming list (n) List showing the names of clients who have booked accommodation, and simple details of any extras that they may require.

ro-ro (abbr.) Roll on, roll off. Car ferry that allows cars to drive on and off. Normally loaded through the stern of the vessel and unloaded from the bows.

roster (n) List of staff and the duties they have to perform at particular times.

rostrum (n) Raised platform on which a speaker stands or sits.

rotation (n) **1** Round trip, made by an aircraft from base to destination and return to base. **2** Moving passengers around in a coach to ensure each one has an opportunity to sit in the best seats.

round the clock (n) In operation or open 24 hours a day.

round trip (n) Outward and return journey.

route (n) **1** Method or direction of travelling between two places. **2** Regularly travelled course or path or direction between two places i.e. bus or coach route. **3** Road (US).

roving mike (n) Microphone that is carried around.

road toll (n) The charge or fee for using a toll road.

R.P.K. (abbr.) Revenue Passenger Kilometres.

R/Q (abbr.) Request.

R.Q. (abbr.) Found on an airline ticket meaning the holder is requested to reconfirm flight.

R.S.A. (abbr.) Royal Society of Arts. Examination body (UK).

R/T (abbr.) Return Trip.

R.T.F. (abbr.) Radiotelephone or Radiotelephony.

R.T.W. Round The World.

rucksack (n) A bag with straps that enables people to put it over their shoulders. It is used by walkers or by climbers. Also known as a pack or backpack (US).

rudder (n) **1** A broad, flat movable piece of wood or metal at the stern (back) of a ship used for steering the ship. **2** Vertical moving surface, attached to the upright fin at the rear of an aircraft (tail), to control the horizontal movement of an aircraft.

runway (n) Landing and take-off surface for aircraft.

R.Y.A. (abbr.) Royal Yachting Association.

Ss - Sierra

S.A. (abbr.) When written on an airline ticket it means the holder must re-confirm the flight booking.

Sabre (n) CRS for American Airlines.

S.A.G.T.A. (abbr.) School & Group Travel Association.

safari (n) A tour or expedition to see or hunt wildlife especially in Eastern and Southern Africa.

safety announcement/briefing (n) Verbal instructions on safety procedures usually given by a crew member of a ship or airliner.

safety deposit box (n) Small lock-up safe provided in hotels, etc. for guests to secure their valuables/money etc.

safety drill (n) When passengers, visitors or guests are told they what have to do in the event of an emergency.

sail (n) **1** Large piece of material attached to the mast of a ship/yacht. When the wind blows against the sail, the ship/yacht will be moved forward. **2** (v) To move a boat/yacht on water. **3** (v) The actual movement of a vessel on water.

salt flat (n) Dried up bed of a salt lake.

salt pan (n) Shallow dip or depression where salty water collects and then is dried out by the sun. The salt that is left is after the water has gone then collected for use elsewhere.

S.A.R. (abbr) Search and Rescue (Air).

S.A.S. (abbr.) Scandinavian Airlines System.

scenic (adj.) Having attractive natural landscape.

schedule (n) Timetable.

scheduled service (n) Regular transport service available to anyone paying a fare.

Schilling (n) Austrian unit of currency.

schuss (v) To ski downhill.

seat pitch (n) Distance between aircraft seats.

sector (n) Defined part of a region, industry or market.

security (n) Procedures to ensure protection and safety of travellers etc.

security screening (n) Machines and trained personnel used to check luggage and passengers before they board transport to ensure that no explosive devices, weapons or other illegal goods are carried on board.

segment (n) Portion or section - usually of a journey.

seat belt (n) Strong, well-anchored adjustable strap used to secure passengers in their seats while in transport.

self-catering (adj.) Accommodation which provides guests with their own cooking facilities.

self employed (adj.) Working independently, directly for clients or customers and not for an employer.

seminar (n) When a group meets for discussion or training.

senior citizen (n) Elderly person or old age pensioner (O.A.P.).

service charge (n) Amount of money added to a bill to cover the cost of waiting staff, usually in a restaurant.

set down (n) Place for passengers to alight from transport.

set meal (n) Meal with no choices of food provided.

setup time (n) Period of time during which an exhibition or conference prepares to open when stands, lighting staging, etc. is arranged.

shell (n) Cover or folder made of paper or stiff board, used to hold leaflets or as front cover of brochure.

shell folder (n) See Shell.

shell scheme (n) Basic stand at an exhibition.

shire (n) Anglo-Saxon English term for administrative district. The person in charge used to be called the Reeve - hence Shire-reeve which later became sheriff.

shore excursion (n) Visit from a cruise ship to land.

shoplifting (n) Illegal act taking goods from a shop without paying for them.

shore (n) The land along the edge of the sea or any large area of water.

shoreline (n) The edge of the sea or any large area of water.

short breaks (n) Holidays that last for a few days only.

short fall (n) The difference between expected and actual business.

shoulder (n) Area at the side of a motorway/highway restricted for emergency use.

shoulder period (n) Period between high and low season.

shuttle (n) Short, frequent, scheduled trips operated by aircraft or coaches; usually no advance reservation is needed.

siesta (n) Traditional custom, particularly in Spain, where the shops are closed during the hottest part of day.

S.I.A. (abbr.) Singapore International Airlines.

sick bag (n) Heavy paper bag carried on transport for passengers to be sick into if they are ill.

sightseeing (n) Tour round a tourist venue or area of interest.

silver service (n) Food service where waiters serve food to each guest at a table using a 'silver' serving spoon and fork.

simultaneous interpreting (n) Translating one language into another while the speaker is speaking.

single (n) **1** Room for one person with one bed. **2** Ticket for one person only. **3** Ticket for a one way or outward journey.

Sirocco (n) Hot dry wind which blows across from Sahara over the South of France

site (n) Area such as park, ruin, Roman settlement etc.

S.I.T.E. (abbr.) Society of Incentive Travel Executives.

site guide (n) Walking tour guide working in park, house or small area.

site inspection (n) Visit to look at facilities, location or venue.

six pm release (n) Around the world hotels will not hold a room after 1800 (6pm) local time if guest has not arrived by this time, unless a special arrangment is made.

ski evolutif (n) Ski training method using very short skis, replacing them with longer skis as the learner progresses or improves.

skipper (n) Captain - usually of a ship or boat or ferry (slang).

skyjack (n) When an airline is hijacked during flight.

slalom (n) Downhill ski race between poles which mark out the course.

sleeper (n) **1** A train with beds for people to use in order to sleep on overnight journeys. **2** A carraige of a train with beds for people to use in order to sleep on overnight journeys.

slide (n) Photographic transparency which can be used in a projector.

slide projector (n) Machine that shines a bright light through a photographic transparency (slide) magnifies this image and projects it onto a screen.

slot (n) The time allocated to an aircraft during which it can take-off.

smart card (n) Plastic card, the same size as a credit card with built-in micro-chip memory that can have many functions.

smart card travel (n) New system where ticket details will be issued and stored electronically on a smart card. The card can then be passed through a machine at the airport instead of waiting at check-in.

smoke hood (n) A hood that is put over a person's head to provide protection against smoke inhalation in the event of a fire.

smuggle (v) To bring, take or send goods into a country secretly and illegally.

smuggler (n) Person who secretly and illegally brings goods into a country. Usually to avoid paying duty or tax or because the goods are illegal.

S.N.A.V. (abbr.) Syndicat National des Agents de Voyages. French Association of Travel Agents.

S.N.C.F. (abbr.) Societé National de Chemins de Fer. French railways organisation.

sniffer dog (n) Dog that is trained to find drugs or explosives etc. by using its sense of smell.

snow cannon (n) Machine that makes and distributes artificial snow.

snow line (n) Level or height on a mountain above which snow is permanent.

social programme (n) Organised social events to entertain people on holiday or people attending a conference.

solar (adj.) From the sun. Solar panels are used in many hotels in Mediterranean countries to generate power to heat water etc.

son et lumiere (n) Sound and Light show at night (Fr).

sommelier (n) Highly trained wine waiter (Fr).

sous chef (n) Assistant to the head chef.

sous vide (n) Food cooked in a central kitchen, away from the serving area, and then reheated before serving.

souvenir (n) Goods bought as gifts etc. that are typical or relate the area where they are bought.

spa (n) Place with a natural water spring.

S.P.A.A. (abbr.) Scottish Passenger Agents Association.

speaker (n) **1** Someone who delivers a talk or speech at a meeting, conference or formal dinner. **2** Part of a sound system from which sound comes.

special interest (n) Holidays catering for people interested in certain subjects or offering specialist lectures

special needs (n) Special requirements for passengers e.g. Disabled passengers have special needs.

speeding (n) When a vehicle is going faster than the speed allowed by law.

split charter (n) When two or more tour companies share the hire of an aircraft.

split shift (n) When staff start work in the morning, go off duty in middle of day, and return to work in the evening - split shifts are often worked in hotels and restaurants.

sponsor (n) Individual or a company giving support, usually financial, to an event.

spot rate (n) Exchange rate that is obtained by making an immediate transfer of currencies.

spotlight (n) Adjustable lights with a beam that can be focused into a small area or spot.

spouse (n) Husband or wife.

spouse events (n) Activities not directly related to a conference normally for entertainment that are part of the spouse programme.

spouse programme (n) Social programme to entertain people that are accompany delegates to a conferance while the conference is in session.

S.P.Q.R. (abbr.) Senatus Populas Que Romanus - for the Roman Senate and the People.

sprinter train (n) Local train service, usually with few carriages, that runs through the countryside connecting major towns and cities.

S.S.S.I. (abbr.) Site of Special Scientific Interest (on a map).

stabiliser (n) Term for exclusive dealing arrangements - i.e. ABTA tour operators may only sell through ABTA retailers who can not sell non-ABTA tour operators' services. Normally this would be illegal, but it has been proved to offer protection for clients' money so it is allowed to continue.

stabilisers (n) Fins below the waterline on the sides of a ship, to stop the ship from rolling in the sea and make a voyage more comfortable for the passengers on board.

stalactite (n) Limestone column hanging from the roof of a cave, formed from calcium carbonate in water as it drips down from the cave roof.

stalagmite (n) Limestone column formed on the floor of a cave from the calcium carbonate in water. The column points up to toward the cave roof.

stall (n) **1** Table or small shop from which things are sold - i.e. market stall.

2 Dangerous loss of speed of an aircraft at which it no longer has enough lift to fly, causing it to fall rapidly.

stalls (n) Seats in a theatre that are nearest the stage.

standby fare (n) Fare that does not guarantee a seat. Passengers with standby tickets can only travel if there are seats available through cancellation or all normal fare paying passengers have been seated and there are still available seats.

stand-by passenger (n) Passengers with no guaranteed seat on transport who wait for a seat to become vacant - e.g. in the event of a booking cancellation a seat will become available.

starboard (n) The right side of a ship or an aircraft when looking from the back toward the front.

starter (n) The first course that is served at a formal meal.

stately home (n) Large house or mansion, usually of historical interest.

stateroom (n) Large and comfortable room or cabin on a ship. Ususally the best and most expensive accommodation on a ship.

station manager (n) **1** Person in charge of a Railway station. **2** Senior staff member of an airline resposible for ground handling at an airport.

status box (n) Section on an airline ticket showing if the ticket is for a confirmed or unconfirmed booking.

sterile (n) Term for an area that has been cordoned off and searched for security reasons. It remains sterile whilst under guard, but if people are let in without being searched, the area loses this status.

stern (n) Back end or rear of a ship.

steward (n) Male member of the crew of a ship or an aircraft who looks after the needs of passengers and serves food etc.

stewardess (n) Female member of the crew of a ship or an aircraft who looks after the needs of passengers and serves food etc.

S.T.O.L. (abbr.) Short Take Off and Landing (aircraft).

stone age (n) Period from about 25000 BC to 20000 BC. First major phase of prehistoric culture, during this time tools and weapons were made from stone.

stow (v) To put away - e.g. luggage.

stowaway (n) Person who travels illegally by hiding on transport.

stowage lockers (n) Closed container shelves used for storing passengers' hand luggage.

strait (n) Narrow stretch of water linking two larger areas of water.

strike (v) When workers refuse to work as a protest.

stop-over (n) Break in a long journey, usually overnight - i.e. when flying from London to Australia many people stop-over in Bangkok or Singapore.

strip cultivation (n) In Europe and UK this was a mediaeval form of farming, where fields were divided into parallel strips.

subcontractor (n) Company or person hired by the principal contractor to help with work.

subsonic (n) Below the speed of sound i.e. subsonic aircraft fly slower than the speed of sound (1225 kph/761mph).

substitute (v) To replace someone who is unable to take up a seat or ticket, etc.

subway (n) **1** U.S. underground or metro system. See underground. **2** A path or passage that allows people to walk under a busy road or under a railway track (UK).

suite (n) Hotel accommodation with a bedroom, bathroom and separate sitting/ living room.

sunbathe (v) To sit or lie outside where the sun shines in order to get a suntan.

sunburn (n) When the skin suffers burning or inflammation from exposure to sun's rays, often causing pain. Sunburn can also be caused by the sun's rays reflecting off water or snow even if the person has not been in direct sunlight.

sun cream/lotion (n) Cream or lotion that gives the skin some protection from the sun and helps to prevent sunburn.

sunglasses (n) Spectacles with dark lenses that protect the eyes from the sun's rays.

sunstroke (n) An illness that is caused by over exposure to heat from the sun.

supersonic (n) Faster than the speed of sound i.e. supersonic aircraft fly faster than the speed of sound (1225 kph/ 761mph).

supplement (n) **1** Additional charge for goods or services. **2** Additional part of a timetable.

supplier (n) Company that provides services or goods.

surcharge (n) Extra or additional charge.

surface (n) Travelling on or by land.

sustainable tourism (n) Tourism that does not interfere with the physical, social and cultural environment of an area.

S.W.B. (abbr.) Single With Bathroom. Single bedroom with en suite bathroom.

Tt - Tango

T (abbr.) When written on airline ticket denotes tourist or economy class.

table d'hôte menu (n) Literally Host's table menu - menu in restaurant or cafe usually with one or few choices and a fixed price.

table plan (n) Diagram showing the location of tables at a function. It usually also shows, in alphabetical order, the names of guests and the tables at which they are sitting.

tacho (abbr.) Tachograph.

tachograph (n) Device for recording distance travelled and the speed of a coach, bus or truck, and also the number of stops the driver makes.

tail wind (n) Wind blowing from behind an aircraft, or other vehicle, making it travel faster.

tailor made (adj.) Holiday designed specially for a specific client.

take off (v) When an aircraft leaves the ground and begins to fly.

Tannoy (n) System of loud speakers used to make public announcements. Public address system (UK).

tariff (n) 1 List of charges. 2 Tax or duty charged by a government on goods being brought into a country.

taxi (n) Car, usually licensed by the local authorities, which can be hired by passengers to take them to a destination.

taxi meter (n) Device in a taxi or cab which measures the cost of a journey.

taxi way (n) Paved area for aircraft movement between the apron and the runway.

T.B.A. (abbr.) To Be Advised.

T.D.A. (abbr.) Timeshare Developers' Association.

T.D.D. (abbr.) Telecommunication Devices for the Deaf.

T.D.H. (abbr.) Table D'Hôte menu.

technician (n) Expert who has a paticular skill or technique, usually mechanical.

T.E.E. (abbr.) Trans Europe Express railway trains.

temp. (abbr.) 1 Temporary. 2 Temporary worker.

temporary (n) 1 Structure that is put up for a short time and will then be dismantled. 2 A member of staff who fills a position for a short period of time and then leaves.

tenant (n) 1 Self-employed person who runs a pub or bar that is owned by a brewery. 2 Person who rents and lives in long term accommodation.

tender (n) 1 Small boat that carries passengers between a larger boat and shore. 2 Formal offer to supply goods or services and a statement of the price that will be charged.

tent (n) Portable shelter, usually made of canvas, that is relatively easy to carry and to erect, to provide overnight accommodation

terminal (n) Building for arrivals and departures- i.e. at an airport or bus depot.

terrace (n) 1 A row of houses adjoining one another by their side walls (UK). 2 A flat area of grass or stone next to a building where people can sit.

T.E.S.A. (abbr.) The Events Suppliers Association.

T.G.V. (abbr.) Train a Grande Vitesse. French high speed train.

theme park (n) Outdoor venue which

is open to the public, that charges an entrance fee and has a theme or special interest.

themed break/holiday (n) Special interest break or holiday.

thermal spring (n) Naturally occurring hot water coming out from the ground.

thin route (n) Airline route where demand for seats is low.

third age (n) Polite term for Old Age Pensioners.

thrust (n) Force from a jet engine or propeller that makes aircraft go forwards.

T.I.A. (abbr.) Travel Industry Association of America.

T.I.C. (abbr.) Tourist Information Centre.

ticket (n) Official piece of paper or card to show that a person can travel on transport, enter a venue or has paid for something in advance.

ticket tout (n) Someone who offers tickets for entry to a popular event at a price higher than the official purchase cost. In US these are known as Scalpers.

tide (n) Regular rise and fall of the sea level, caused by the attraction of the moon and sun. This happens twice every 24 hours.

time share (n) Holiday accommodation that is owned by several people who can use it at different times of the year.

timetable (n) Schedule of events or travel times.

time zone (n) Area of the world where the time is calculated as being a particular number of hours ahead or behind GMT. These areas are usually across 15° of longitude.

T.I.M.G. (abbr.) Tourist Industry Marketing Group.

tip (n) Gratuity given for good service.

toastmaster (n) Person at formal functions that announces the names of guests as they arrive, and has other ceremonial duties including the calling for silence so that guests can make speaches and propose toasts . In UK they often wear a uniform with a red tailcoat and white bow tie.

T.O.C. (abbr.) Tour Operators' Council of ABTA.

toilet (n) Lavatory or W.C.

toll (n) Charge or fee for using a toll road or a toll bridge.

tonnage (n)weight measurement for the carrying capacity of a ship.

tornado (n) Violent wind storm at the centre of which is a funnel shaped cloud.

T.O.S.G. (abbr.) Tour Operators' Study Group.

tour conductor (n) Tour Manager in charge of a group.

tour director (n) Person in charge of group of tourists. Level 4 N.V.Q. advanced qualification.

tour guide (n) Person in charge of coach group. Level 2 N.V.Q. basic qualification.

tour manager (n) Person in charge of coach group. Level 3 N.V.Q. intermediate qualification.

tour operator (n) Company that organises and manages package tours.

tourism (n) Temporary movement of people to destinations outside the places where they normally live and work, and their activities during their stay at these destinations.

tourist (n) Someone who spends a night away from home on holiday or business. Person who visits another area or country generally for a holiday or pleasure, but certain tourist statistics will include visits for business and medical treatment.

tourist board (n) Official office for promotion of a city, region or country.

tourist class (n) Least expensive class for air travel.

townhouse hotel (n) Type of hotel offering luxury accommodation in renovated domestic buildings.

T.Q.M. (abbr.) Total Quality Management.

trade fair/show (n) Exhibition confined to people working in a specific industry or association that is not open to the general public.

Trade Descriptions Act 1968 (n) Legislated act making it illegal to make false or misleading claims about a product or service that could deceive purchasers (UK).

traffic manager (n) Person in a coach company responsible for the day-to-day running and allocation of coaches.

trail (n) **1** Designated route through the countryside. **2** Walking tour, with a theme, in a town or city .

Tramontana (n) Cold dry wind blowing south starting from northern Italy and central Spain.

transfer **1** (v) Move passengers from one location to another. **2** (n) Ticket that allows passengers to continue their journey on another train or bus (US).

transhumance (n) A traditional event,which involves moving animals such as sheep between different seasonal grazing grounds. Today this is very rare, but it used to take place in France and Spain when flocks were moved from their winter quarters to higher summer pastures.

transport **1** (n) Vehicle or craft used to take people or goods from one place to another. **2** (v) to take people or goods from one place to another.

transit (n) The process of being taken or moving between one place to another.

transit passengers (n) Passengers waiting for a connecting flight to their final destination.

translator (n) Person who changes the spoken or written word from one language into another language.

transport officer (n) Person in charge of travel arrangements.

travel agent (n) Company selling holidays and travel tickets direct to the public on behalf tour operators and transport companies.

travel agency (n) Retail shop that sells holidays, business travel tickets, and tour packages.

travel trade manual (n) Book or booklet issued by a tourist board or large hotel group, giving basic information useful when organising tours. Travel trade manuals are issued to the tourism industry only and not to the general public.

traveller (n) Person who goes from one place to another.

traveller's cheque (n) Cheque bought from a bank or travel agent that can easily be exchanged for cash at another bank or bureau de change etc. while travelling abroad. Traveller's cheques are a safe way of carrying money, as issuing banks usually guarantee to replace them if the cheques are stolen. Invented originally by Thomas Cook.

travel document (n) Issued by Home Office to a person who has no official nationality and therefore no passport. This document allows them to travel internationally but they will have to get a visa for all the countries to which they wish to travel (UK).

Travicom (n) Air flight information and reservation computer terminal system.

trek (n) Special interest holiday with much of the travelling done on foot or by a form of basic transport such as truck or lorry.

trip (n) Journey or tour.

triple (n) Room with three beds.

trolley (n) Small wheeled vehicle used by porters or passengers to transport luggage.

tropics (n) Area of the world, which normally has warm weather. The tropics are located between the Tropic of Cancer latitude 23° and 30 minutes North, and the Tropic of Capricorn 23° and 30 minutes South.

tronc (n) Central collection for tips and gratuities in restaurant or hotel.

tropical rain forest (n) Forests found in the tropical areas of the world which contain a wide variety of plant and animal life. At the present time there is international concern for these forests many of which are being cut down for timber and cleared for farming. This destroys the area and causes erosion, and some scientists think that the hydrology and natural balance of the earth may be altered if all the equatorial rain forest is destroyed.

T.S.S.A. (abbr.) Transport Salaried Staffs Association.

T.T.C. (abbr.) The Timeshare Council.

T.W.B. (abbr.) Twin With Bath. Room with two beds and a bathroom.

twenty-four hour clock (n) System of time measurement which runs from 0001 (12:01am) to 2400 (12:00 pm) each day.

turbulence (n) Violent or uneven movement in a particular section of air. This can cause aircraft to be shaken or jolted while in flight.

tundra (n) Barren Arctic plains of northern Canada and Eurasia.

turnstile (n) A metal gateway with revolving central post that will only admit one person at a time.

turn round/around (n) Time allocated between passengers getting leaving an aircraft or a ship and it being ready to receive the next group of passengers.

turnpike (n) Toll road (US).

twin (n) Twin room, room with two beds.

twinning (n) When a town forms a social arrangement with another town in another country.

typhoon (n) A violent tropical storm.

Uu - Uniform

U.F.T.A.A. (abbr.) Universal Federation of Travel Agents' Associations.

U.H.F. (abbr.) Ultra-High Frequency.

U.L. (abbr.) Unlicensed (alcohol not served).

U.M. (abbr.) Unaccompanied Minor.

unaccompanied minor (n) Child or young person travelling alone.

unconfirmed (n) Not officially agreed.

undercut (v) Selling goods or sevices at a lower price than other organisations, usually unofficially.

undertow (n) A current in the sea flowing the opposite way to the surface current, usually away from the shore. Undertow may be dangerous to swimmers as it can take them out to sea.

U.D.P. (abbr.) Unitary Development Plan. Proposals that local councils have to submit to Department of the Environment every ten years setting out their plans for tourism and environmental development (UK).

undercarraige (n) The part of an aircraft that supports it when it is on the ground. This would include the wheels.

underground (n) The name of the London railway system that is situated below the ground.

UNESCO (acr.) United Nations Educational, Scientific and Cultural Organisation

Unfair contract terms (n) Legislated Act for consumer protection. The Unfair Contract Terms Act 1977 determines the extent to which parties or companies can limit their liability through existing contracts in cases where negligence is proved (UK).

uniform (n) Official clothes provided by an organisation for employees or representatives to wear when working to give a unified image and to make them easily identifiable.

unlimited (adj.) Without a limit, any amount or quantity is available.

Union Flag (n) Correct name for the flag of the United Kingdom. The term Union Jack should only be used when the flag is flying from the bows of a ship.

unpressurised (n) When the air inside an aircraft is not pressurised.

upgrade (v) **1** Move to more expensive or superior seats or accomodation. **2** (n) Seats, accomodation or services of a higher standard are provided at no extra charge.

up-market (n) Term for expensive and/ or good quality.

urban (adj.) Living, or situated in a city or town.

U.S.P. (abbr.) Unique selling point - positive aspect of goods or services used in their promotion or marketing.

U.S.T.S. (abbr.) United States Travel Service. Official US agency for promotion of tourism to the USA.

Vv - Victor

V (abbr.) Symbol for vegetarian choice on menu.

vacate (v) Leave accommodation, seat etc. making it available for other people to use.

vacant (adj.) Empty, not being used.

vacancy (n) **1** Job or position that is available. **2** Accommodation that is available.

vacation (n) Holiday.

vacationer (n) Holiday-maker (US).

vaccine (n) Substance containing a harmless form of germs that cause a particular disease. This substance is introduced into the body to produce immunity from that particular disease.

vaccination (n) The process of introducing the vaccine into a body, usually by injection.

valet (n) Member of staff in a hotel who looks after the clothes of male guests.

valid (adj.) Acceptable to authority and effective for the intended purpose.

validate (v) To make something valid.

validation (n) Confirmation to ensure something is valid.

validity (n) Period of time for which something is valid.

VAT (abbr.) Value Added Tax.

V.C.R. (abbr.) Video Cassette Recorder.

vehicle (n) Something that is used for transport of people or goods usually on land - i.e. a car, coach, etc.

veld/veldt (n) Wild, uncultivated grassland in South Africa.

venue (n) Place that people agree to meet usually that has facilities for conferences, meetings or that has entertainment.

venue inspection (v) Visit made by organisers before an event to check on the facilities etc.

veranda (n) A raised platform that is situated along the side of some houses where people can sit. Some verandas have roofs.

verger (n) A church official in the UK, who could be likened to a 'house-keeper', looking after the church and helping the Vicar in their duties. n.b. At St. Paul's Cathedral they are called Virgers.

verify (v) To check or confirm that something is accurate or correct.

V.F.R. (abbr.) Visiting Friends and Relatives.

V.H.F. (abbr.) Very High Frequency. Radio broadcasting frequency between 30 - 300 MHz.

via 1 (preposition) To go through a place on the way to a destination. **2** (n) Italian for road.

viaduct (n) Bridge of short spans supported on piers or towers, that carries a railway or road across a valley.

vicar (n) The priest of a parish; a church official who takes church services and administers to the needs of the local people (UK).

vice versa (preposition) The other or opposite way round to that which has been stated.

video cassette (n) A sealed cartridge containing magnetic tape (video tape) used for recording sounds and pictures. These sounds and pictures can to be shown on a television using a video player.

video conferencing (n) System using video cameras connected by telephone lines, enabling people to see and talk to each other, even if they are separated by a long distance.

video player (n) Equipment which plays or reads video cassettes or tapes and displays sounds and pictures stored on them on a television or monitor.

video recorder (n) Equipment for recording sounds and pictures on to video cassettes or tape.

video tape (n) Long flexible Magnetic strip (tape) used for recording sounds and pictures which can later be played back or read using a video player.

view line (n) Eye level of each member of the audience, in relation to the stage.

villa (n) Large house, usually a house where people stay while on holiday.

village (n) Small settlement or collection of houses, generally with a church and shops.

V.I.P. (abbr.) Very Important Person.

visa (n) Official stamp or paper in a passport, to show the holder can enter or leave a foreign country.

visibility (n) The extent to which the light or weather enables people to see things from a distance.

visit 1 (v) To go to a place venue or country for a short time (not perma-nently) for the purposes of recreation or business. **2** (n) The period of time or act of visiting.

visitor (n) Person who goes to a place, venue or country for a short time (not permanently) for the purposes of recreation or business.

visitor attraction (n) Venue opened for tourist visits.

visitor centre (n) Reception area that gives visitors tourist information about a geographical area, museum or other place of interest.

volcano (n) Mountain through which molten lava, gas, ash etc. from under the surface of the earth bursts out or erupts. Volcanoes can be dormant or 'dead' and so are unlikely to erupt.

volume (n) The amount or quantity of something - i.e. volume of traffic.

voucher (n) Ticket given as a receipt for payment which the holder can use instead of money to obtain specified goods or services.

Voyage (n) Journey on a ship.

V.S.T.O.L. (abbr.) Vertical Short Take-off and Landing aircraft.

V.T.O.L. (abbr.) Vertical Take-off and Landing aircraft.

V.V.V. (abbr.) Tourist Information Centres in the Netherlands.

Ww - Whisky

wadi (n) Valley, stream or riverbed in the Middle East which is generally dry, but after rain becomes the main channel for water.

Wagons-Lit (n) Name of the company that operates sleeping accommodation on European trains.

wait listed (adj.) Passengers on a waiting list for an aircraft flight that is already fully booked.

waitress (n) Woman employed to serve customers food at their table in a restaurant.

waiter (n) Man employed to serve customers food at their table in a restaurant.

wake up call (n) See Alarm call.

walking tour (n) Guided tour travelling by or on foot.

Warsaw Convention (n) Convention held in 1929 to establish an agreement on the extent of liability for death, injury or loss of luggage that an airline has to its passengers. The Warsaw Convention currently limits compensation payments to relatively low amounts however, moves are being made to raise the limit.

W.A.T.A. (abbr.) World Association of Travel Agencies.

water park (n) Recreation area with water sports and other water based activities.

water taxi (n) Small motor boat used to transport people.

waybill (n) List of goods or passengers being transported.

weekend (n) Days at the end of the working week when businesses are normally shut.

weekend break (n) Short holiday the duration of which is a weekend.

welcome (n) To greet in a friendly way.

welcome cocktail (n) Drinks served to visitors on their arrival so that they can all meet each other.

welcome meeting (n) Where a tour operators' representatives (Reps.) welcome clients to a resort, give them introduction to the resort and what activities and excusions are available.

wetland (n) Marsh or damp uncultivated land.

wet lease (n) Where an aircraft is leased with crew.

wharf (n) Platform or structure next to a river or to the sea where ships berth. Often used as an loading/unloading area for passengers and cargo.

whispered interpreting (n) Simultaneous interpreting in a low voice to one or two persons seated adjacent to the interpreter.

white board (n) A shiny white board on which a lecturer or speaker can draw or write using special pens, so that the board can be cleaned afterwards.

white tie (adj.) This refers to a white bow tie worn by men at an event requiring formal clothing. and long evening dress for women. See also black tie.

W.H.O. (abbr.) World Health Organization.

wholesaler (n) Tour operator - often one who sells to companies and not directly to the public.

wide-bodied jet (n) Air/aeroplane with extra wide body that has more seats than a normal air/aeroplane.

wildlife park (n) Place where animals

are kept in simulated natural surroundings so that they can be viewed by the public.

wind-chill factor (n) The cooling effect on the skin of wind, especially at low temperatures.

windsurfer (n) **1** A board similar to a surfboard with a sail. **2** Person who sails a windsurfer on water.

wine waiter (n) Waiter who serves wine to customers in a restaurant.

wings (n) **1** The long flat parts of an aircraft that stick out of the side that support it while in flight. The engines are usually attached to them. **2** The part of a building that sticks out from the main part - usually associated with large houses, hospitals etc. **3** The part of the stage that is hidden from the audience-theatres, conferences etc.

W/L (abbr.) Wait Listed.

workshop (n) **1** Meetings, usually held around small tables, to enable participants to share their knowledge and experience through a series of discussions and practical work. **2** Place where craftsmen work which contains their tools etc.

world heritage site (n) UNESCO defined sites of natural, historical, or conservational importance around the world.

W.T.O. (abbr.) World Tourism Organisation.

W.T.T. (abbr.) World Travel and Tourism Council.

Xx - X-ray

xenophobia (n) Strong dislike or fear of foreigners or non-natives.

Xmas (Abbr.) Christmas.

X-ray (n) Radiation that can pass through most solid materials. Machines that use X-rays are used to check the contents of luggage, especially at airports, for illegal or dangerous goods. X-rays are also used to examine broken bones and other internal injuries.

Yy - Yankee

Y (abbr.) Economy Class.

yacht (n) Boat or small ship used for pleasure.

yellow card (n) Internationally acknowledged record of vaccination and immunisation against disease.

Yen (n) Japanese unit of currency.

Y.H.A. (abbr.) Youth Hostel Association.

Y.M.C.A. (abbr.) Young Men's Christian Association. - A hostel for men administered by the Y.M.C.A.

youth (n) Young person, usually less than 26 years old.

youth hostel (n) Inexpensive accommodation, that often includes dormitories, for young people or those travelling on a small budget.

Y.W.C.A. (abbr.) Young Women's Christian Association. - A hostel administered by the Y.W.C.A. organisation where women can stay.

Zz - Zulu

zero (n) Naught, Nill, Null or 0.

zero-rated (n) No tax applies to items which are zero rated - i.e. no VAT payable (UK).

zone (n) **1** A defined area of earth's surface - i.e. time-zone. **2** A defined area such as secure area of an airport.

zoo (n) Display of animals that is open to the public.

Hotel foyer

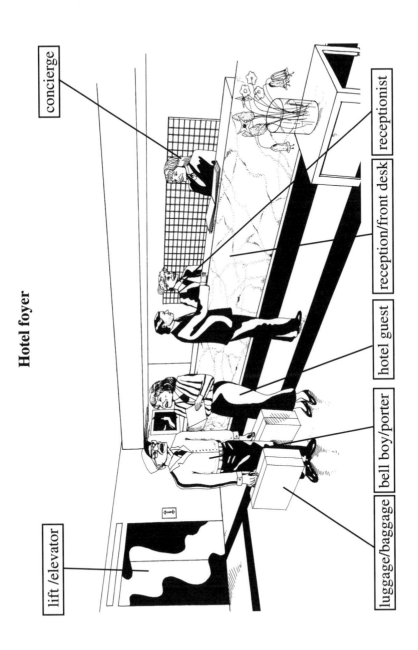

concierge

receptionist

reception/front desk

hotel guest

bell boy/porter

luggage/baggage

lift /elevator

Beach

sail

mast

winsurfer

deck chair

sunbather

parosol

hot air balloon

Apron of an airport

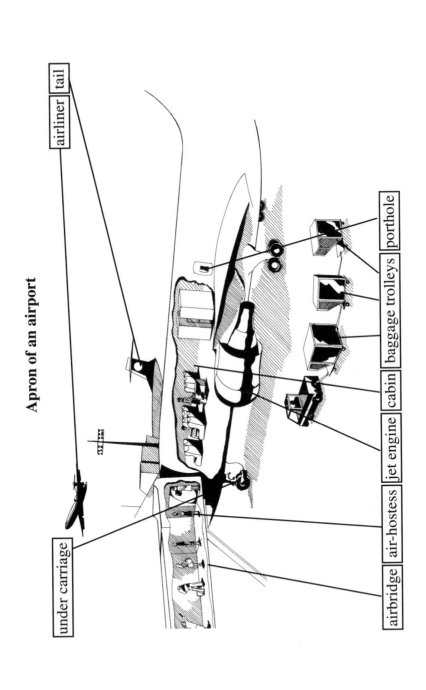

airliner | tail

under carriage

porthole

baggage trolleys

cabin

jet engine

air-hostess

airbridge

Train station

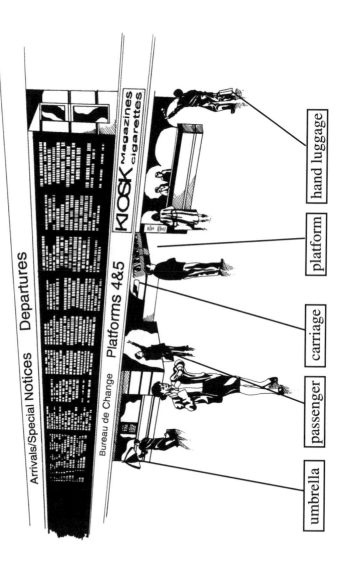

Arrivals/Special Notices   Departures

Bureau de Change   Platforms 4&5

KIOSK Magazines cigarettes

umbrella   passenger   carriage   platform   hand luggage

Countries of the World

In this section, you will find a list of the majority of the countries of the world. Under each country, there are six important facts that we thought relevant for the different users of this dictionary. There are two other pieces of information that we would like to have included for each of the countries listed, one being currency exchange rates and the other being time bands in relation to Greenwich Mean Time (G.M.T.). We decided not to enter the exchange rates due to the volatility and weakness of some of these countries and their relative currencies, that to publish them, would be a gross inaccuracy. The time bands, we believe, will change in the near future, as British time may be altered

AFGANISTAN
Capital - Kabul
Language.- Pushtu, Dari
Currency - Afghani
Religions - Musim, Sunni (Persian)
Climate - Continental
Int. Dialling Code - Int.+ 93
ALBANIA
Capital - Tirana
Languages - Albanian, Greek
Currency - Lek
Religion - Muslim
Climate - Mediterrannean
Int. Dialling Code - Int. + 355
ALGERIA
Capital - Algiers
Languages - Arabic, Berber, French
Currency - Dinar
Religion - Muslim
Climate - South of Country is very hot,
North (Coast)Mediterranean
Int. Dialling Code - Int. + 213
ANDORRA
Capital - Andorra-la-Vella
Languages - French, Spanish
Currencies - French Franc, Spanish
Paseta
Religion - Roman Catholic
Climate - Winter is severe, Summer is
cool and sunny
Int. Dialling Code - Int. + 33628
ANGOLA
Capital - Luanda
Languages - Portuguese and African
Languages
Currency - Kwanza
Religions - Roman Catholic, Protestant
Climate - Tropical
Int. Dialling Code - Int. + 244
ANTIGUA AND BARBUDA
Capital - St. John's
Language - English
Currency - East Caribbean Dollar
Religion - Christian

Climate - Tropical
Int. Dialling Code - Int. + 1809
ARGENTINA
Capital - Buenos Aires
Languages - Spanish (Official), Eng-
lish, French, Italian,German
Currency - Peso
Religion - Roman Catholic
Climate - North is subtropical, South
is subarctic
Int. Dialling Code - Int. + 54
AUSTRALIA
Capital - Canberra
Language - English
Currency - Australian Dollar
Religion - Anglican, Roman Catholic,
Protestant
Climate - Hot and Dry
Int. Dialling Code - Int. + 61
AUSTRIA
Capital - Vienna
Language - German
Currency - Schilling
Religions - Roman Catholic, Protes-
tant
Climate - Continental
Int. Dialling Code - Int. + 43
BAHAMAS
Capital - Nassau
Language - English, Carribean Creole
Currency - Bahamian Dollar
Religions - Anglican, Baptist, Roman
Catholic
Climate - Subtropical and Mild
Int. Dialling Code - Int. + 1809
BAHRAIN
Capital - Manama
Languages - Arabic (Official), English,
Farsi, Urdu
Currency - Bahrain Dinar
Religion - Muslim
Climate - Very Dry, Very Hot in Sum-
mer and also very humid
Int. Dialling Code - Int. + 973

BANGLADESH
Capital - Dhaka
Languages - Bengali, English
Currency - Taka
Religions - Sunni Muslim, Hindu
Climate - Tropical
Int. Dialling Code - Int. + 880

BARBADOS
Capital - Bridgetown
Language - English
Currency - Barbados Dollar
Religion - Anglican
Climate - Subtropical
Int. Dialling Code - Int. + 1809

BELGIUM
Capital - Brussels
Languages - Flemish in the north of the country, Walloon (French) in the south of the country
Currency - Belgian Franc
Religion - Roman Catholic
Climate - Temperate
Int. Dialling Code - Int. + 32

BOLIVIA
Capital - La Paz
Language - Spanish and Local Languages
Currency - Boliviano
Religion - Roman Catholic
Climate - Tropical. On higher ground it is cooler
Int. Dialling Code - Int. + 591

BOTSWANA
Capital - Gabarone
Language - English, Setswana
Currency - Pula
Religions - Christian, Tribal
Climate - Subtropical and Dry
Int. Dialling Code - Int. + 267

BRAZIL
Capital - Brasillia
Language - Portuguese and numerous Indian Languages
Currency - Cruzado

Religion - Roman Catholic
Climate - Tropical and Subtropical
Int. Dialling Code - Int. + 55

BRUNEI
Capital - Bandar Seri Begawan
Language - Mostly Malay (Official), Chinese, English
Currency - Brunei Dollar
Religion - Muslim, Confucianist, Buddhist, Taoist
Climate - Tropical - very humid and wet
Int. Dialling Code - Int. + 673

BULGARIA
Capital - Sofia
Language - Bulgarian, Turkish
Currency - Lev
Religion - Eastern Orthodox Christian
Climate - Continental in north of country and in the mountains, Mediterranean in the south.
Int. Dialling Code - Int. + 359

CAMBODIA
Capital - Phnom Penh
Language - Khmer (Official), French
Currency - Cambodian Riel
Religion - Therevada Buddhist
Climate - Tropical. Monsoon from April to October.
Int. Dialling Code - Int + 855

CAMEROON
Capital - Yaounde
Language - French, English, Tribal (Various African Languages)
Currency - African Financial Community Franc
Religion - Roman Catholic, Muslim, Tribal (Various African Religions)
Climate - Tropical
Int. Dialling Code - Int. + 237

CANADA
Capital - Ottawa
Language - English, French
Currency - Canadian Dollar
Religion - Roman Catholic, Protestant

Climate - Arctic in the north, Continental
Int. Dialling Code - Int. + 1
CHILE
Capital - Santiago
Language - Spanish
Currency - Peso
Religion - Roman Catholic
Climate - Desert in the north, Arctic in the south
Int. Dialling Code - Int. + 56
CHINA
Capital - Beijing
Language - Chinese (Mandarin-official, Cantonese and variations of these two dialects)
Currency - Yuan
Religion - Confucianist, Muslim, Taoist, Buddhist
Climate - Temperate and Humid in the south and the central south. Dry in the north.
Int. Dialling Code - Int. + 86
COLOMBIA
Capital - Bogota
Language - Spanish
Currency - Peso
Religion - Roman Catholic
Climate - Tropical, Temperate on the plateaux
Int. Dialling Code - Int. + 57
COSTA RICA
Capital - San Jose
Language - Spanish
Currency - Colon
Religion - Roman Catholic
Climate - Tropical, Temperate on the plateaux
Int. Dialling Code - Int. + 506
CROATIA
Capital - Zagreb
Language - Croatian variant of Serbo-Croatian
Currency - Croatian Dinar

Religion - Roman Catholic (Croats), Orthodox Christian (Serbs)
Climate - Continental in the north, Mediterranean in the south.
Int. Dialling Code - Int. + 385
CUBA
Capital - Havana
Language - Spanish
Currency - Cuban Peso
Religion - Roman Catholic
Climate - Subtropical
Int. Dialling Code - Int. + 53
CYPRUS
Capital - Larnaca
Language - Greek and Turkish (Official), English
Currencies - Cyprus Pound, Turkish Lira
Religion - Greek Orthodox
Climate - Mediterranean
Int. Dialling Code - Int. + 357
CZECH REPUBLC
Capital - Prague
Language - Czech
Currency - The new Krown / Koruna
Religion - Mainly Roman Catholic
Climate - Continental - hot summers and cold winters
Int. Dialling Code - Int. + 42
DENMARK
Capital - Copenhagen
Language - Danish
Currency - Kroner
Religion - Lutheran
Climate - Maritime
Int. Dialling Code - Int. + 45
DOMINICA
Capital - Roseau
Language - English
Currencies - East Carribean Dollar, Pound Sterling, French Franc
Religion - Roman Catholic
Climate - Subtropical
Int. Dialling Code - Int. + 1809

DOMINICAN REPUBLIC
Capital - Santo Domingo
Languange - Spanish
Currency - Peso
Religion - Roman Catholic
Climate - Subtropical and Maritime Tropical
Int. Dialling Code - Int. + 1809

ECUADOR
Capital - Quito
Language - Spanish, Various Indian Languages
Currency - Sucre
Religion - Roman Catholic
Climate - Tropical, cooler on higher ground
Int. Dialling Code - Int. + 593

EGYPT
Capital - Cairo
Language - Arabic
Currency - Egyptian Pound
Religion - Muslim
Climate - Hot an Dry
Int. Dialling Code - Int. + 20

EL SALVADOR
Capital - San Salvador
Language - Spanish
Currency - Colon
Religion - Roman Catholic
Climate - Subtropical, much cooler on the higher ground
Int. Dialling Code - Int. + 503

ESTONIA
Capital - Tallinn
Language - Estonian (Finnish extraction)
Currency - Kroon
Religion - Lutheran
Climate - Temperate, cold winters
Int. Dialling Code - Int. + 372

ETHIOPIA
Capital - Addis Ababa
Language - Amharic
Currency - Birr

Religion - Ethiopian Christian, Sunni Muslim
Climate - Hot on the low ground, Temperate on the higher Ground
Int. Dialling Code - Int. + 251

FIJI
Capital - Suva
Language - English (Offical), Hindi, Fijian
Currency - Fiji Dollar
Religion - Hindu, Methodist
Climate - Tropical
Int. Dialling Code - Int. + 679

FINLAND
Capital - Helsinki
Language - Finnish and Swedish
Currency - Markka
Religion - Lutheran
Climate - Temperate, very cold winters
Int. Dialling Code - Int. + 358

FRANCE
Capital - Paris
Language - French
Currency - French Franc
Religion - Roman Catholic
Climate - Temperate, Dry and Hot summers on the mediterranean coast - the south of the country
Int. Dialling Code - Int. + 33

GABON
Capital - Libreville
Language - French (Official), various African languages
Currency - African Financial Community Franc - CFA Franc
Religion - Christian
Climate - Tropical
Int. Dialling Code - Int. + 241

GAMBIA
Capital - Banjul
Languages - English (Official), Various African Languages
Currency - Dalasi
Religion - Muslim

Climate - Tropical
Int. Dialling Code - Int. + 220
GERMANY
Capital - Berlin
Language - German
Currency - Deutsche mark
Religion - Protestant, Roman Catholic
Climate - Continental - Temperate
Int. Dialling Code - Int. + 49
GHANA
Capital - Accra
Language - English (Official), various African languages
Currency - Cedi
Religion - Christian, Muslim, Tribal-various African religions
Climate - Tropical
Int. Dialling Code - Int. + 233
GREECE
Capital - Athens
Language - Greek
Currency - Drachma
Religion - Greek Orthodox
Climate - Mediterranean
Int. Dialling Code - Int. + 30
GRENADA
Capital - St. George's
Language - English
Currency - East Carribean Dollar
Religion - Christian, Roman Catholic
Climate - Subtropical
Int. Dialling Code - Int. + 1809
GUATEMALA
Capital - Guatemala City
Languages - Spanish, various Indian languages.
Currency - Quetzal
Religion - Roman Catholic, Protestant
Climate - Subtropical, Temperate on the higher ground
Int. Dialling Code - Int. + 502
GUYANA
Capital - Georgetown
Languages - English (Official), Hindi,

Urdu, various local languages
Currency - Guyanese Dollar
Religion - Christian, Hindu, Urdu
Climate - Tropical
Int. Dialling Code - Int. + 592
HAITI
Capital - Port-au-Prince
Languages - French, Creole-Carribean English
Currency - Gourde
Religion - Roman Catholic, Christian, Voodoo
Climate - Tropical
Int. Dialling Code - Int. + 509
HONDURAS
Capital - Tegucigalpa
Languages - Spanish (Official), English, various Indian languages
Currency - Lempira
Religion - Roman Catholic
Climate - Tropical
Int. Dialling Code - Int. + 504
HONG KONG
Capital - Victoria
Languages - English, Chinese
Currency - Hong Kong Dollar
Religion - Buddhist, Taoist
Climate - Subtropical, monsoon season from May to September
Int. Dialling Code - Int. +852
HUNGARY
Capital - Budapest
Languages - Hungarian (Magyar)
Currency - Forint
Religion - Roman Catholic
Climate - Continental
Int. Dialling Code - Int. + 36
ICELAND
Capital - Reykjavik
Languages - Icelandic
Currency - Krona
Religion - Lutheran
Climate - Temperate
Int. Dialling Code - Int. + 354

INDIA
Capital - New Delhi
Languages - Hindi, English, also numerous other languages such as Bengali, Urdu, Tamil, Punjabi
Currency - Rupee
Religion - Hindu. Also numerous other religions such as Muslim, Sikh, Christian, Buddhist, Jain
Climate - Tropical, monsoon season from June to September.
Int. Dialling Code - Int. + 91

INDONESIA
Capital - Jakarta
Languages - Indonesian
Currency - Rupiah
Religion - Muslim, also Christian, Buddhist, Hindu
Climate - Equatorial
Int. Dialling Code - Int. +62

IRAN
Capital - Tehran
Language - Farsi (Official)
Currency - Rial
Religion - Shi'ite Muslim (Official)
Climate - Continental
Int. Dialling Code - Int. + 98

IRAQ
Capital - Baghdad
Languages - Arabic (Official), also Kurdish, Turkish, Assyrian
Currency - Iraqi Dinar
Religion - Muslim
Climate - Very Hot Summers, cool winters
Int. Dialling Code - Int. + 964

IRELAND
Capital - Dublin
Language - English, Irish Gaelic (Both Official)
Currency - Punt
Religion - Roman Catholic
Climate - Temperate
Int. Dialling Code - Int. + 353

ISRAEL
Capital - Jerusalem
Language - Hebrew and Arabic (Both Official)
Currency - Shekel
Religion - Judaism
Climate - Subtropical
Int. Dialling Code - Int. + 972

ITALY
Capital - Rome
Language - Italian
Currency - Lira
Religion - Roman Catholic
Climate - Mediterranean
Int. Dialling Code - Int. + 39

JAMAICA
Capital - Kingston
Language - English, Spanish, Jamaican Creole
Currency - Jamaican Dollar
Religion - Roman Catholic, Rastafarian
Climate - Tropical on sea level, temperate on higher ground (mountains)
Int. Dialling Code - Int. + 1809

JAPAN
Capital - Tokyo
Language - Japanese
Currency - Yen
Religion - Shinto, Buddhist - Shintoism, Christian
Climate - Monsoon climate
Int. Dialling Code - Int. + 81

JORDAN
Capital - Amman
Languages - Arabic (Official), English
Currency - Jordanian Dinar
Religion - Sunni Muslim, Christian
Climate - Hot and Dry, cool in the winter.
Int. Dialling Code - Int. + 962

KENYA
Capital.- Nairobi
Language - Swahilli (Official), English

and various African languages
Currency - Kenya Shilling
Religion - Christian, various African
Muslim religions
Climate - Tropical, temperate inland
Int. Dialling Code - Int. + 254
KOREA, NORTH
Capital - Pyongyang
Language - Korean
Currency - Won
Religion - Buddhist, Confucianist
Climate - Continental
Int. Dialling Code - Int. + 850
KOREA, SOUTH
Capital - Seoul
Language - Korean
Currency - Won
Religion - Buddhist, Christian, Confucianist
Climate - Continental
Int. Dialling Code - Int + 82
KUWAIT
Capital - Kuwait City
Language - Arabic, Farsi, Kurdish,
English
Currency - Kuwaiti Dinar
Religion - Muslim
Climate - Hot and Dry
Int. Dialling Code - Int. + 965
LAOS
Capital - Vientiane
Languages - Lao (Official), French
Currency - New Kip
Religion - Buddhist
Climate - Tropical, monsoon season
May to October
Int. Dialling Code - Int. + 856
LEBANON
Capital - Beirut
Language - Arabic, French (Both Official), English, Armenian
Currency - Lebanese Pound
Religions - Muslim, Christian
Climate - Subtropical

Int. Dialling Code - Int. + 961
LESOTHO
Capital - Maseru
Language - English, Sesotho (Both
Official), Zulu, Xhosa
Currency - Maluti
Religion - Protestant, Roman Catholic
Climate - Continental
Int. Dialling Code - Int. + 266
LIBYA
Capital - Tripoli
Language - Arabic
Currency - Libyan Dinar
Religion - Muslim
Climate - Hot and Dry
Int. Dialling Code - Int. + 218
LIECHTENSTEIN
Capital - Vaduz
Language - German
Currency - Swiss Franc
Religion - Roman Catholic, Protestant
Climate - Temperate
Int. Dialling Code - Int. + 4175
LUXEMBOURG
Capital - Luxembourg City
Language - French (Official), German,
Letzeburgesh-A spoken language, not
a written language
Currency - Luxembourg Franc
Religion - Roman Catholic
Climate - Temperate
Int. Dialling Code - Int. + 352
MADAGASCAR
Capital - Antananarivo
Languages - Malagasy (Official),
French, English
Currency - Malagasy Franc
Religion - Tribal- various religions,
Christian, Muslim
Climate - Tropical
Int. Dialling Code - Int. + 261
MALAYSIA
Capital - Kuala Lumpar
Languages - Malay (Official),

Currency - Rinngit
Religion - Muslim (Official), Buddhist
Climate - Tropical, monsson season from October to February in the east, monsson season from May to September in the west.
Int. Dialling Code - Int. + 60
MALDIVES
Capital - Male
Languages - Divehi - Sinhalese Dialect, English
Currency - Rufiya
Religion - Muslim
Climate - Tropical, monsoon season from June to August
Int. Dialling Code - Int. + 960
MALTA
Capital - Valletta
Language - English, Maltese
Currency - Maltese Lira
Religion - Roman Catholic
Climate - Mediterranean
Int. Dialling Code - Int. + 356
MAURITIUS
Capital - Port Louis
Language - English (Official), French, Ctreole, various Indian languages
Currency - Mauritius Rupee
Religion - Hindu, Christian, Muslim
Climate - Subtropical
Int. Dialling Code - Int. + 230
MEXICO
Capital - Mexico City
Language - Spanish (Official)
Currency - Peso
Religion - Roman Catholic
Climate - Tropical on lower ground, Temperate on higher ground
Int. Dialling Code - Int. + 52
MONACO
Capital - Monaco-Ville
Language - French (Official)
Currency - French Franc
Religion - Roman Catholic

Climate - Mediterranean
Int. Dialling Code - Int. + 3393
MONGOLIA
Capital - Ulan Bator
Language - Mongolian (Official), Chinese, Russian
Currency - Tugrik
Religion - Buddhist, but officially none
Climate - Dry and Cold
Int. Dialling Code - Int. + 976
MOROCCO
Capital - Rabat
Language - Arabic (Official), Berber, French, Spanish
Currency - Dirham
Religion - Muslim
Climate - Warm
Int. Dialling Code - Int. + 212
MYANMAR - Formerly known as Burma
Capital - Yangon - Formerly known as Rangoon
Language - Burmese
Currency - Kyat
Religion - Buddhist
Climate - Tropical, monsoon season from May to September
Int. Dialling Code - Int. + 95
NAMIBIA
Capital - Windhoek
Language - Afrikaans, English, German, also several other African languages
Currency - South African - Rand
Religion - Lutheran, Roman Catholic, Christian
Climate - Very Dry
Int. Dialling Code - Int. + 264
NEPAL
Capital - Katmandu
Language - Nepali (Official), numerous other local languages
Currency - Nepalese Rupee
Religion - Hindu

Climate - Temperate
Int. Dialling Code - Int. + 977
NETHERLANDS
Capital - Amsterdam
Language - Dutch
Currency - Guilder
Religion - Roman Catholic, Protestant
Climate - Temperate
Int. Dialling Code - Int. + 31
NEW ZEALAND
Capital - Wellington
Language - English (Official), Maori
Currency - New Zealand Dollar
Religion - Protestant, Roman Catholic
Climate - Temperate
Int. Dialling Code - Int. + 64
NICARAGUA
Capital - Managua
Language - Spanish (Official), Indian, English
Currency - Cordoba
Religion - Roman Catholic
Climate - Tropical
Int. Dialling Code - Int. + 505
NIGERIA
Capital - Lagos
Languages - English (Official), Hausu, Ibo, Yoruba
Currency - Naira
Religion - Muslim, Christian
Climate - Subtropical
Int. Dialling Code - Int. + 234
NORWAY
Capital - Oslo
Language - Norwegian (Official)
Currency - Krone
Religion - Lutheran
Climate - Temperate, cold in the north of the country
Int. Dialling Code - Int. + 47
OMAN
Capital - Muscat
Language - Arabic (Official), English
Currency - Rial Omani

Religion - Muslim
Climate - Hot summer, Mild winter
Int. Diallling Code - Int. + 968
PAKISTAN
Capital - Islamabad
Language - Urdu and English (Both Official), Punjabi, other languages as well
Currency - Pakistan Rupee
Religion - Muslim
Climate - Subtropical, monsoon season from June to October
Int. Dialling Code - Int. + 92
PANAMA
Capital - Panama City
Languages - Spanish (Official), English
Currency - Balboa
Religion - Roman Catholic
Climate - Tropical
Int. Dialling Code - Int. + 507
PAPUA NEW GUINEA
Capital - Port Moresby
Languages - English (Official), Tok Pisin-Pidgin English,literally hundreds of other languages-700 approx.
Currency - Kina
Religion - Christian
Climate - Tropical
Int. Dialling Code - Int. + 675
PARAGUAY
Capital - Ascuncion
Languages - Spanish (Official), Guarani
Currency - Guarani
Religion - Roman Catholic
Climate - Subtropical
Int. Dialling Code - Int. + 595
PERU
Capital - Lima
Languages - Spanish, Quechua (Both Official)
Currency - New Sol
Religion - Roman Catholic

Climate - Temperate, cooler on higher ground
Int. Dialling Code - Int. + 51
PHILIPPINES
Capital - Manila
Languages - Tagalog-Philipino (Official), English, Spanish
Currency - Philippine Peso
Religion - Roman Catholic
Climate - Tropical
Int. Dialling Code - Int. + 63
POLAND
Capital - Warsaw
Language - Polish (Official), German
Currency - Zloty
Religion - Roman Catholic
Climate - Temperate
Int. Dialling Code - Int. + 48
PORTUGAL
Capital - Lisbon
Language - Portuguese
Currency - Escudo
Religion - Roman Catholic
Climate - Hot and Dry summers, mild and damp winters
Int. Dialling Code - Int. + 351
PUERTO RICO
Capital - San Juan
Language - Spanish, English
Currency - U.S. Dollar
Religion - Roman Catholic
Climate - Subtropical
Int. Dialling Code - Int. + 1809
QATAR
Capital - Doha
Language - Arabic (Official), English
Currency - Qatar Riyal
Religion - Muslim
Climate - Hot, cooler in the winter
Int. Dialling Code - Int. + 974
ROMANIA
Capital - Bucharest
Language - Romanian
Currency - Leu

Religion - Romanian Orthodox
Climate - Continental
Int. Dialling Code - Int. + 40
RUSSIA
Capital - Moscow
Language - Russian
Currency - Rouble
Religion - Mainly Russian Orthodox
Climate - Continental, arctic in the north
Int. Dialling Code - Int. + 7
ST. LUCIA
Capital - Castries
Languages - English, French Patois
Currency - East Carribean Dollar
Religion - Roman Catholic
Climate - Subtropical
Int. Dialling Code - Int. + 1809
ST. VINCENT AND THE GRENADINES
Capital - Kingston
Languages - English, French Patois
Currency - East Carribean Dollar
Religion - Christian
Climate - Subtropical, dry season January to May
Int. Dialling Code - Int. + 1809
SAN MARINO
Capital - San Marino
Language - Italian
Currency - Italian Lira
Religion - Roman Catholic
Climate - Mediterranean
Int. Dialling Code - Int. + 39549
SAUDI ARABIA
Capital - Riyadh
Language - Arabic
Currency - Rial
Religion - Muslim
Climate - Hot and Dry
Int. Dialling Code - Int. + 966
SEYCHELLES
Capital - Victoria
Language - Creole, French, English (all

Official)
Currency - Seychelles Rupee
Religion - Roman Catholic
Climate - Tropical
Int. Dialling Code - Int. + 248
SINGAPORE
Capital - Singapore City
Language - Malay, Chinese, English, Tamil (All Official)
Currency - Singapore Dollar
Religion - Buddhist, Christian, Muslim, Hindu, Taoist,- Multi religious
Climate - Equatorial
Int. Dialling Code - Int. + 65
SLOVAK REPUBLIC
Capital - Bratislava
Language - Slovak (Official)
Currency - New Koruna
Religion - Roman Catholic, Lutheran
Climate - Continental, hot summers and cold winters
Int. Dialling Code - Int. + 42
SLOVENIA
Capital - Ljubljana
Language - Slovene
Currency - Tolar
Religion - Roman Catholic
Climate - Continental
Int. Dialling Code - Int. + 386
SOUTH AFRICA
Capital - Pretoria
Language - Afrikaans, English (Both Official)
Currency - Rand
Religion - Christian, Muslim, Hindu,and tribal religions
Climate - Temperate
Int. Dialling Code - Int. + 27
SPAIN
Capital - Madrid
Language - Spanish
Currency - Peseta
Religion - Roman Catholic
Climate - Mediterranean in the south

and on the east coast, temperate everywhere else
Int. Dialling Code - Int. + 34
SRI LANKA
Capital - Colombo
Language - Sinhala, Tamil, English
Currency - Sri Lankan Rupee
Religion - Buddhist, Hindu, Muslim, Christian
Climate - Tropical
Int. Dialling Code - Int. + 94
SWEDEN
Capital - Stockholm
Language - Swedish
Currency - Krona
Religion - Lutheran
Climate - Hot summers, cold winters
Int. Dialling Code - Int. + 46
SWITZERLAND
Capital - Bern
Language - German, French, Italian
Currency - Swiss Franc
Religion - Roman Catholic, Protestant
Climate - Warm summers, Cold winters
Int. Dialling Code - Int. + 41
SYRIA
Capital - Damascus
Language - Arabic
Currency - Syrian Pound
Religion - Muslim
Climate - Very Hot and Dry inland, Mediterranean on the coast
Int. Dialling Code - Int. + 963
TAIWAN
Capital - Taipei
Language - Mandarin Chinese (Official), other Chinese dialects
Currency - New Taiwan Dollar
Religion - Confucianist, Buddhist
Climate - Subtropical
Int. Dialling Code - Int. + 886
TANZANIA
Capital - Dar es Salam

Language - Kiswahili, English (Both Official)
Currency - Tanzanian Shilling
Religion - Tribal, Muslim, Christian
Climate - Tropical
Int. Dialling Code - Int. + 255

THAILAND
Capital - Bangkok
Language - Thai, Chinese (Both Official)
Currency - Baht
Religion - Buddhist
Climate - Tropical, monsoon season from May to October
Int. Dialling Code - Int. + 66

TRINIDAD AND TOBAGO
Capital - Port of Spain
Language - English (Official)
Currency - Trinidad and Tobago Dollar
Religion - Roman Catholic, Hindu, Protestant
Climate - Tropical
Int. Dialling Code - Int. + 1809

TUNISIA
Capital - Tunis
Language - Arabic (Official), French
Currency - Dinar
Religion - Muslim
Climate - Hot and Dry inland, Temperate on the coast
Int. Dialling Code - Int. + 216

TURKEY
Capital - Ankara
Language - Turkish (Official), Arabic, Kurdish
Currency - Turkish Lira
Religion - Muslim
Climate - Mediterranean
Int. Dialling Code - Int. + 90

UGANDA
Capital - Kampala
Language - English (Official), Luganda, Lwo, Swahili, Ateso

Currency - Uganda New Shilling
Religion - Roman Catholic, Protestant, Muslim
Climate - Tropical, cooler on the higher ground
Int. Dialling Code - Int. + 256

UKRAINE
Capital - Kiev
Language - Ukrainian
Currency - Grivna
Religion - Ukrainian Orthodox
Climate - Temperate
Int. Dialling Code - Int. + 380

UNITED ARAB EMIRATES
Capital - Abu Dhabi
Language - Arabic (Official)
Currency - United Arab Emirates Dirham
Religion - Muslim
Climate - Hot, cool in the winter
Int. Dialling Code - Int. + 971

UNITED KINGDOM
Capital - London
Language - English
Currency - Pound Sterling
Religion - Christian (Roman Catholic and Protestant)
Climate - Temperate
Int. Dialling Code - Int. + 44

UNITED STATES OF AMERICA
Capital - Washington DC
Language - English, Spanish
Currency - US Dollar
Religion - Christian-Roman Catholic, Methodist, Baptist, Lutheran
Climate - Subtropical in the south, Hot summers and Cold winters in the north
Int. Dialling Code - Int. + 1

URUGUAY
Capital - Montevideo
Language - Spanish
Currency - Nuevo Peso
Religion - Roman Catholic
Climate - Temperate

Int. Dialling Code - Int. + 598
VATICAN CITY STATE
Capital - Vatican City
Language - Latin (Official), Italian
Currency - Vatican City Lira, Italian Lira
Religion - Roman Catholic
Climate - Mediterranean
Int. Dialling Code - Int. + 39
VENEZUELA
Capital - Caracas
Language - Spanish (Official)
Currency - Bolivar
Religion - Roman Catholic
Climate - Tropical
Int. Dialling Code - Int. + 58
VIETNAM
Capital - Hanoi
Language - Vietnamese (Official)
Currency - Rial
Religion - Buddhist
Climate - Tropical
Int. Dialling Code - Int. + 84
YEMEN
Capital - San'a
Language - Arabic
Currency - Rial
Religion - Muslim
Climate - Hot and Humid
Int. Dialling Code - Int. + 967
ZAMBIA
Capital - Lusaka
Language - English (Official), local languages
Currency - Kwacha
Religion - Christian
Climate - Tropical
Int. Dialling Code - Int. + 260
ZIMBABWE
Capital - Harare
Language - English (Official), Shona, Sindebele

Currency - Zimbabwe Dollar
Religion - Christian, Muslim, Hindu
Climate - Subtropical
Int. Dialling Code - Int + 263

CLIMATE DEFINITIONS

Tropical - High temperatures and heavy rainfall throughout the

Subtropical - High temperatures throughout the year in association with extremely varied rainfall, particularly associated with monsoon regions of the world.

Hot - Temperatures that exceed 100 degrees and where rainfall is less than 10 inches / 250 mm per year.

Mediterranean - Hot and dry summers, mild moist winters.

Temperate - Rainfall and temperature are evenly distributed throughout the year, but the day to day weather of a country with a temperate climate is extremely changeable.

Equatorial - Always warm and moist.

Monsoon - Rain at one part of the year and a dry season at the other part of the year. Temperatures range more widely, especially in the dry season.

Continental - The summers are hot and the winters are very cold. The summers bring rain and thunderstorms, and the winters bring frost and varying amounts of snow.

Arctic - Variable climate. The summer months (May to July) brings quiet, overcast and sometimes foggy weather. The temperatures at the height of the summer (July) can get to freezing or just above freezing. The autumn is the most variable season with snow and gales.

Weights and Measures

I n this small section, you will find a list of conversion tables for calcu lating weights and measures, that people associated with the travel and tourism industry may encounter.

KEY:
oz = ounce / ounces
g = gram / gramme / grammes
Kg = Kilogram / Kilogramme
Kgs = Kilogrammes
lb = pound
lbs = pounds
Km = Kilometre(s)
in = inch
mm = millimetre / millimeter
ft = foot / feet
m = metre / meter

WEIGHT

1 oz= 28.35g
1g= 0.04oz

1lb= 0.45Kgs
1Kg= 2.20lbs

1 Ton = 1.02 Tonnes
1 Tonne = 0.98 Tons

DISTANCE

I Mile = 1.61 km
1 km = 0.62 Miles

LENGTH

1 in = 25 mm
1 ft = 305 mm
10 ft = 3.05 m
10 mm = 0.394 in
1m = 3.281 ft

AREA

1 Acre = 0.405 Hectares
1 Hectare = 2.471 Acres

CAPACITY

1 USA fluid oz = 0.030 metric litre
1 imperial fluid oz = 0.028 metric litre
8 USA fluid oz = 1/2 Pint
10 imperial fluid oz = 1/2 Pint
16 USA fluid oz = 1 Pint
20 Imperial fluid oz = 1 Pint
2 Pints = 1 Quart
1 Quart = 0.946 metric litre
1 Quart = 1.137 metric litres
4 Quart = 1 USA Gallon
4 Quart = 1 Imperial Gallon
1 USA Gallon = 3.785 metric litres
1 Imperial Gallon = 4.546 metric litres

Airport and Airline codes

Eighty percent of the travel and tourism industry is either directly or indirectly associated with air travel. The modern airliners / aircraft can now travel such long distances, and due to the enormous competition for passengers among the ever increasing number of carriers, airline travel is becoming more and more affordable for more and more people travelling to more and more different destinations throughout the world. It is with this in mind, that we have, therefore, published a list of the airline codings of the major airlines and their respective countries' of origin, and the airport codings and their respective cities'.

AIRLINE CODINGS -
The major airlines of the world

Key: * = National Flag Carrier

A
AA American Airlines (US)
AC Air Canada *
AF Air France*
AH Air Algerie*
AI Air India*
AM Aeromexico*
AN Ansett Australian Airlines
AO Aviaco (Spain)
AR Aerolineas Argentinas*
AT Royal Air Maroc (Morocco)*
AV Avianca (Colombia)*
AY Finnair (Finland)*
AZ Alitalia (Italy)*

B
BA British Airways*
BB Balair (Switzerland)
BD British Midland
BG Biman Bangladesh Airlines*
BI Royal Brunei Airlines*
BP Air Botswana*
BR EVA Airlines (Taiwan)
BU Braathens (Norway)
BW BWIA - British West Indian Airlines (Trinidad and Tobago)*

C
CA Air China
CI China Airlines
CK Gambia Airlines*
CO Continental Airlines (USA)
CU Cubana (Cuba)*
CX Cathay Pacific (Hong Kong)
CY Cyprus Airways*

D
DL Delta Airlines (USA)
DM Maersk Air (Denmark)
DP Air 2000 (UK)
DS Air Senegal*
DY Alyemda - Yemen Airlines (South Yemen)*
D6 Inter Air (UK)

E
EI Air Lingus*
EK Emirates (United Arab Emirates)*
EL Air Nippon (Japan)
ET Ethiopian Airlines*

F
FF Tower Air (USA)
FI Icelandair*
FR Ryanair (Ireland)
FV Viva Air (Spain)

G
GA Garuda Indonesia*
GF Gulf Air (Bahrain)
GH Ghana Airways*
GU Aviateca (Guatemala)*

H
HA Haiwaian Airlines*
HM Air Seychelles*
HP America West Airlines (USA)
HV Transavia Airlines (The Netherlands)

I
IB Iberia (Spain)*
IC Indian Airlines
IR Iran Air*
IT Air Inter (France)
IY Yemenia - Yemen Airlines (North Yemen)*

J
JD Japan Air System
JE Manx Air (UK)
JK Spanair (Spain)

JL   JAL-Japan Airlines*
JP   Adria Airlines (Slovenia)

K

KA   Dragonair (Hong Kong)
KE   Korean Air (South Korea)
KJ   British Mediterranean Airways
KL   KLM - Royal Dutch Airlines
(The Netherlands)
KM   Air Malta
KQ   Kenya Airways*
KU   Kuwait Airways*
KX   Cayman Airways*

L

LA   LAN - Chile*
LG   Luxair (Luxembourg)*
LH   Lufthansa (Germany)*
LO   LOT - Polish Airlines*
LT   L.T.U. International Airlines
(Germany)
LX   Crossair (Switzerland)
LY   El Al Israel Airlines*
LZ   Balkan (Bulgaria)*
L6   Air Maldives*

M

MA   MALEV Hungarian Airlines*
ME   MEA - Middle East Airlines
(Lebanon)*
MH   Malaysia Airlines*
MJ   LAPA (Paraguay)*
MK   Air Muritius*
MP   Martinair (The Netherlands)
MS   Egyptair*
MX   Mexicana Airlines (Mexico)

N

NG   Lauda Air (Austria)
NH   All Nippon Airways (Japan)
NW   North West Airlines (USA)
NZ   Air New Zealand*

O

OA   Olympic Airways (Greece)*
OK   CSA - Czechoslovak Airlines*
OM   MIAT - Mongolian Airlines*

OS   Austrian Airlines*
OU   Croatia Airlines*
OV   Estonia Air*

P

PG   Pakistan International Airlines*
PL   Aeropreu*
PR   Philippine Airlines*

Q

QF   Qantas Airways (Australia)*
QU   Uganda Airlines*

R

RA   Royal Nepal Airlines*
RB   Syrian Arab Airlines*
RG   VARIG (Brazil)*
RJ   Royal Jordanian Airlines*
RK   Air Afrique
RO   TAROM (Romania)*

S

SA   South African Airways*
SD   Sudan Airways*
SK   SAS - Scandanavian Air
Systems*
SN   Sabena Belgian World Airlines*
SQ   Singapore Airlines*
SR   Swisssair (Switzerland)*
SU   Aeroflot (Russia)*
SV   Saudia (Saudia Arabia)*
SW   Air Namibia*

T

TA   Taca International Airlines (El
Salvador)*
TG   Thai Airways International*
TK   Turkish Airlines*
TP   TAP Air Portugal*
TQ   Transwede Airways (Sweden)
TU   Tunis Air (Tunisia)*
TW   TWA (USA)
TZ   America Trans Air (USA)

U

UA   United Airlines (USA)
UK   Air UK
UM   Air Zimbabwe*

US   US Air (USA)
UX   Air Europa
V
VA   VIASA (Venezuela)*
VD   Air Liberte (France)
VN   Vietnam Airlines*
VS   Virgin Atlantic (UK)
W
WG   Taiwan Airlines
WH   China North West Airlines
WN   Southwest Airlines (USA)
WO   World Airways (USA)
WT   Nigeria Airways*
X
X2   China Xinhua Airlines
Y
YK   Cyprus Turkish Airlines
YP   Aero Lloyd (Germany)
Z
ZB   Monarch Airlines (UK)
ZQ   Ansett New Zealand
Z9   Aero Zambia*

AIRPORT / CITY CODINGSS - The major airports and cities throughout the world.

A
AAH-Aarhus-Denmark
ABQ-Albuquerque-USA
ABS-Abu Simbel-Egypt
ACE-Lanzarote-Canary Islands
ADB-Izmir-Turkey
ADD-Addis Ababa-Ethiopia
ADE-Aden-South Yemen

ADL-Adelaide-Australia
AEP-Buenos Aires-Argentina
AGA-Agadir-Morocco
AGP-Malaga-Spain
AIY-Atlantic City-USA
AKL-Aukland-New Zealand
ALB-Albany, New York-USA
ALC-Alicante-Spain
ALG   Algiers-Algeria
AMM   Amman-Jordan
AMS-Amsterdam-The Netherlands
ANC-Anchorage, Alaska   USA
ANK-Ankara-Turkey
ANR-Antwerp-Belgium
ANU-Antigua-Leeward Islands, West Indies
AQJ-Aqaba-Jordan
ARN-Stockholm-Sweden
ASE -Aspen, Colorado-USA
ASU-Asuncion-Paraguay
ATH-Athens-Greece
ATL-Atlanta, Georgia-USA
AUH-Abu Dhabi-United Arab Emirates
AYQ-Ayers Rock-Australia
B
BAH-Bahrain-Bahrain
BAJ-Bali-Papua New Guinea
BBU-Bucharest-Romania
BCN-Barcelona-Spain
BDA-Bermuda-Bermuda
BEY-Beirut-Lebanon
BFS-Belfast-United Kingdom
BG-Barbados-Barbados, West Indies
BGO-Bergen-Norway
BHX-Birmingham-United Kingdom
BHZ-Belo Horizonte-Brazil
BIO-Bilbao-Spain
BJL-Banjul-Gambia
BJS-Beijing-China
BKK-Bangkok-Thailand
BLL-Billund-Denmark
BLQ-Bologna-Italy
BLR-Bangalore-India

BMA-Stockholm, Bromma-Sweden
BNE-Brisbane-Australia
BNJ-Bonn-Germany
BOD-Bordeaux-France
BOG-Bogota-Colombia
BOM-Bombay-India
BOS-Boston, MA-USA
BRE- Bremen-Germany
BRI-Bari-Italy
BRN-Berne-Switzerland
BRQ-Brno-Czech Republic
BRS-Bristol-United Kingdom
BRU-Brussels-Belgium
BSB-Brasilia-Brazil
BSL-Basle-Switzerland
BTS-Bratislava-Slovak Republic
BUD-Budapest-Hungary
BUE-Buenos Aires-Argentina
BUH-Bucharest-Romania
BWI-Baltimore, MD-USA
BWN-Bandar Seri Begawan-Brunei

C

CAG-Cagliari-Italy (Sicily)
CAI-Cairo-Egypt
CAS-Casablanca-Morocco
CBR-Camberra-Australia
CCU-Calcutta-India
CGH-Sao Paulo-Brazil
CGK-Jakarta-Indonesia
CGN-Cologne-Germany
CIA-Rome (Ciampino)-Italy
CLE-Cleveland, OH-USA
CLT-Charlotte, NC-USA
CMB-Colombo-Sri Lanka
CMN-Casablanca-Morocco
CNF-Belo Horizonte-Brazil
CNS-Cairns-Australia
COR-Cordoba-Argentina
CPH-Copenhagen-Denmark
CPT-Cape Town-South Africa
CUN-Cancun-Mexico
CVG-Cincinnati, OH-USA
CWL-Cardiff-UK
CXH-Vancouver-Canada

D

DAC-Dhaka-Bangladesh
DAM-Damascus-Syria
DAR-Dar-es-Salaam-Tanzania
DEL-Delhi-India
DEN-Denver, CO-USA
DFW-Dallas F/W, TX-USA
DHA-Dhahran-Saudi Arabia
DLM-Dalaman -Turkey
DOH-Dohar-Qatar
DRS-Dresden-Germany
DRW-Darwin-Australia
DTM-Dortmund-Germany
DTT-Detroit, MI-USA
DUB-Dublin-Ireland
DUR-Durban-South Africa
DUS-Dusseldorf-Germany
DXB-Dubai-United Arab Emirates

E

EAB-San Sebastian-Spain
EBB-Entebbe (Kampala)-Uganda
EDI-Edinburgh-United Kingdom
EIN-Eindhoven-The Netherlands
ELP-El Paso, TX-USA
EMA-East Midlands-United Kingdom
EWR-New York/ Newark-USA
EYW-Key West, FL-USA

F

FAO-Faro-Portugal
FCO-Rome L da V-Italy
FIH-Kinshasa-Zaire
FLL-Fort Lauderdale, FL-USA
FLR-Florence-Italy
FMO-Munster-Germany
FNA-Freetown-Sierra Leone
FNC-Funchal-Medeira
FNJ-Pyongyang-North Korea
FPO-Freeport-Bahamas
FRA-Frankfurt-Germany

G

GCI-Guernsey-United Kingdom
GM-Grand Cayman-Cayman Islands
GDL-Guadalajara-Mexico

GDN-Gdansk-Poland
GEO- Georgetown-Guyana
GIB-Gibraltar-Gibraltar
GIG-Rio de Janeiro-Brazil
GLA-Glasgow-United Kingdom
GNB-Grenoble-France
GOA-Genoa-Italy
GOT-Gothenburg-Sweden
GRU-Sao Paulo-Brazil
GRX-Granada-Spain
GRZ-Graz-Austria
GUA-Guatemala City-Guatemala
GVA-Geneva-Switzerland
GWY-Galway-Ireland
GYE-Guayaquil-Ecuador

H

HAJ-Hanover-Germany
HAM-Hamburg-Germany
HAN-Hanoi-Vietnam
HAV-Havana-Cuba
HBA-Hobart (Tasmania)-Australia
HDD-Hyderabad-Pakistan
HEL-Helsinki-Finland
HER-Heraklion (Crete)-Greece
HFA-Haifa-Israel
HIJ-Hiroshima-Japan
HKG-Hong Kong (Kai Tak)-Hong Kong
HKT-Phuket-Thailand
HND-Tokyo (Haneda)-Japan
HNL-Honolulu, HI-USA
HOU-Houston, TX-USA
HRE-Harare-Zimbabwe

I

IAD-Washington (Dulles)-USA
IBZ-Ibiza-Spain
IEV-Kiev-Ukraine
IND-Indianapolis, IN-USA
INN-Innsbruck-Austria
INV-Inverness-United Kingdom
IOM-Isle of Man-United Kingdom
ISB-Islamabad-Pakistan
IST-Istanbul-Turkey

ITM-Osaka (Itami)-Japan
IZM-Izmir-Turkey

J

JAX -Jaxonville, FL-USA
JED-Jeddah-Saudi Arabia
JER-Jersey-United Kingdom
JFK-New York (JFK)-USA
JIB-Djibouti-Djibouti
JKT-Jakarta-Indonesia
JNB-Johannesburg-South Africa
JRS-Jerusalem-Israel
JSI-Skiathos-Greece

K

KGL-Kigali-Rwanda
KGS-Kos-Greece
KHI-Kirachi-Pakistan
KIN-Kingston-Jamaica
KIX-Osaka (Kansai)-Japan
KRK-Krakow-Poland
KTM-Katmandu-Nepal
KUL-Kuala Lumpar-Malaysia
KWI-Kuwait-Kuwait

L

LAD-Luanda-Angola
LAS-Las Vegas-USA
LAX-Los Angeles-USA
LBA-Leeds/Bradford-United Kingdom
LBV-Libreville-Gabon
LCA-Larnaca-Cyprus
LCY-London City-United Kingdom
LDY-Londonderry-United Kingdom
LED-St. Petersburg-Russia
LEH-Le Havre-France
LEI-Almeira-Spain
LEJ-Leipzig-Germany
LFW-Lome-Togo
LGA-New York (La Guardia) USA
LGB-Long Beach, CA-USA
LGG-Liege-Belgium
LGW-London Gatwick-United Kingdom
LHE-Lahore-Pakistan

LHR-London Heathrow-United Kingdom
LIL-Lille-France
LIM-Lima-Peru
LIN-Milan (Linate)-Italy
LIS-Lisbon-Portugal
LJU-Ljubljana-Slovenia
LNZ-Linz-Austria
LOS-Lagos-Nigeria
LPA-Gran Canaria-Canary Islands
LPB-La Paz-Bolivia
LPL-Liverpool-United Kingdom
LTN-London Luton-United Kingdom
LUG-Lugano-Switzerland
LUN-Lusaka-Zambia
LUX-Luxembourg-Luxembourg
LXR-Luxor-Egypt
LYP-Faisalabad-Pakistan
LYS-Lyon-France

M

MAA Madras-India
MAD-Madrid-Spain
MAH-Menorca-Spain
MAN-Manchester-United Kingdom
MBA-Mombasa-Kenya
MBJ-Montego Bay-Jamaica
MCI-Kansas City-USA
MCO-Orlando-USA
MCT-Muscat-Oman
MDE-Medellin-Colombia
MEL-Melbourne-Australia
MEM-Memphis-USA
MEX-Mexico City-Mexico
MGQ-Mogadishu-Somalia
MIA-Miami-USA
MIR-Monastir-Tunisia
MJV-Murcia-Spain
MKE-Milwaukee-USA
MLH-Mulhouse-France
MLW-Monrovia-Liberia
MME-Teeside-United Kingdom
MMX-Malmo-Sweden
MNI-Montserrat-Montserrat
MNL-Manila-Philippines

MPL-Montpellier-France
MRS-Marseille-France
MRU-Mauritius-Mauritius
MSP-Minneapolis, MN-USA
MSQ-Minsk-Belarus
MST-Maastricht-The Netherlands
MSY-New Orleans, LA-USA
MTY-Monterrey-Mexico
MUC-Munich-Germany
MVD-Montevideo-Uruguay
MXP-Milan (Malpensa)-taly

N

NAP-Naples-Italy
NAS-Nassau-Bahamas
NBO-Nairobi-Kenya
NCE-Nice-France
NCL-Newcastle-UnitedKingdom
NGO-Nagoya-Japan
NGS-Nagasaki-Japan
NRT-Tokyo (Narita)-Japan
NTE-Nantes-France
NTY-Sun City-South Africa
NUE-Nuremberg-Germany

O

OAK-Oakland, CA-USA
ODE-Odense-Denmark
OKA-Okinawa-Japan
OKC-Oklahoma City-USA
OKD-Sapporo-Japan
OPO-Porto-Portugal
ORD-Chicago (O'Hare)-USA
ORY-Paris (Orly)-France
OTP-Bucharest (Otopeni)-Romania

P

PAP-Port au Prince-Haiti
PEK-Beijing-China
PEN-Penang-Malaysia
PER-Perth-Australia
PGF-Perpignan-France
PHL-Philadelphia, PA-USA
PHX-Phoenix, AZ-USA
PIK-Glasgow (Prestwick) United Kingdom

PIT-Pittsburgh, PA-USA
PMF-Parma-Italy
PMI-Palma de Mallorca-Spain
PMO-Palermo-Italy
PNM-Phnom-Penh-Cambodia
POM-Port Moresby-Papua New Guinea
POS-Port of Spain-Trinidad and Tobago
PSA-Pisa-Italy
PTY-Panama City (Tocumen)-Panama

R

RBA-Rabat -Morocco
REC-Recife-Brazil
RHO-Rhodes-Greece
RIX-Riga-Latvia
RKV-Reykjavik-Iceland
RMI-Rimini-Italy
RTM-Rotterdam-The Netherlands
RUH-Riyadh-Saudi Arabia

S

SAH-Sana'a-North Yemen
SAL-San Salvador-El Salvador
SAN-San Diego, CA-USA
SAT-San Antonio,-TX-USA
SCL-Santiago-Chile
SDQ-Santa Domingo-Dominican Republic
SDR-Santander-Spain
SDU-Rio deJaneiro-Brazil
SDV-Tel Aviv-Israel
SEA-Seattle, WA-USA
SEL-Soeul (Kimpo)-South Korea
SFO-San Francisco, CA-USA
SGN-Ho Chi Minh City-Vietnam
SIN-Singpore-Singapore
SJO-San Jose-Costa Rica
SJU-San Juan-Puerto Rico
SKG-Thessaloniki-Greece
SOF-Sofia-Bulgaria
SSA-Salvador-Brazil
STN-London (Stansted)-United Kingdom

STR-Stuttgart-Germany
SVG-Stavanger-Norway
SVO- Moscow (Sheremetyevo)-Russia
SVQ-Seville-Spain
SXB-Strasbourg-France
SXF-Berlin (Schonefeld)-Germany
SYD-Sydney-Australia
SZG-Salzburg-Austria

T

TFN-Tenerife-(Norte)-Canary Islands
TFS-Tenerife-(Reina Sofia)-Canary Islands
TGU-Tegucigalpa-Honduras
THF-Berlin (Tempelhof)-Germany
THR-Tehran-Iran
TIA-Tirana-Albania
TKS-Tokushima-Japan
TLL-Tallin-Estonia
TLS -Toulouse-France
TLV-Tel Aviv (Ben Gurion) Israel
TNG-Tangier-Morocco
TNR-Antananarivo-Madagascar
TPA-Tampa, FL-USA
TPE-Taipei (Kai Chek)-Taiwan
TRN-Turin-Italy
TUL-Tulsa, OK-USA
TUN-Tunis-Tunisia
TUS-Tuscon, AZ-USA
TXL-Berlin (Tegel)-Germany

U

UIO-Quito-Ecuador
ULN-Ulan Bator-Mongolia
UME-Umea-Sweden

V

VCE-Venice-Italy
VLC-Valencia-Spain
VNO-Vilnius-Lithuania
VRN-Verona-Italy

W

WAW-Warsaw-Poland
WDH-Windhoek-Namibia
WLG-Wellington-New Zealand

X
XRY-Jerez-Spain
Y
YEG-Edmonton-Canada
YHZ-Halifax-Canada
YMX-Montreal (Mirabel)-Canada
YOW-Ottawa-Canada
YUL-Montreal (Dorval)-Canada
YVR-Vancouver-Canada
YYC-Calgary-Canada
YYJ-Victoria-Canada
YYZ-Toronto-Canada
Z
ZAG-Zagreb-Croatia
ZAZ-Zaragoza-Spain
ZRH-Zurich-Switzerland

Fillers

When touring the United Kingdom, or working with English speaking groups, passengers and tourists often ask Guides and Tour Managers to explain the meaning of expressions, some of which are very strange! In the following section, you will find a small list of the most common expressions used and some possible explanations.

"ACHILLES HEEL": "soft and vulnerable spot".
Originates from the story when Thesis took her son **Achilles** by the **heel**, and immersed him in the river Styx to make him invulnerable. She held him at the ankle which wasn't covered and protected, so this was his one weak spot and eventually he was slain by an arrow piercing him in the **heel**
Today it can be used to highlight a **weak spot** in a company's plan or tour.

"BACK TO SQUARE ONE": "To go back/return and start all over again"
Comes from the early days of broadcasting before television, when, to make it easier to follow a football match listening to the radio commentary, a numbered grid diagram of a pitch was published in radio programmes, so listeners could follow matches more easily. **Square One** was the centre where teams kicked off and returned to each time a goal was scored

"BEYOND THE PALE": Originates from Dublin, Ireland. In the14th Century people living beyond the **stakes (pales)** were considered to be uncivilised. **Beyond the stakes/pales** means beyond the boundaries of the town/city, so anyone who did not live in Dublin, and therefore, lived in the countryside, was regarded as inferior.

"BLUESTOCKING": "Someone who is intelligent but boring" Mrs. Elizabeth Montague, who lived in Portman Square, London, had an English language club and she liked to invite some of the most intelligent people to her club. One of the most regular people was Benjamin Stillingfleet who wore **bluestockings**, so the other members of the club were nicknamed **'bluestockings'**.

"BOB'S YOUR UNCLE": When something is easy to do because of family or friendly influence.
The original **'Bob'** was the politician A. J. Balfour, who was given Government positions by his uncle, who was the Prime Minister Robert, Lord Salisbury.

"BOYCOTT": "To stop dealings with a person, group or firm". This word originates from Ireland. The Land League of Ireland prevented anyone from dealing with a land owner called **Captain Boycott.** The Land League of Ireland said that any person that had dealings with **Captain Boycott** would be ignored.

"BRAND NEW": "Very new".
Originates from the word **brand** which means to burn. In the old days a metal object **new** from an iron forge was still burning hot.

"BURNING THE CANDLE AT BOTH ENDS": "When a person works hard in the day and socialises a lot at night". Another phrase for this is **"To work hard and to play hard"**
Originates from the time when poor people made lights by dipping rushes into grease which they bent in the middle and lit at both ends, to give double the light.

"BUTTONHOLE": When one person talks to another and the person being talked to can't leave, even if they want to.

Originates from the days when men had **buttonholes** in their jacket lapels, and one person would hold another by the lapel or **buttonhole**, so they could not leave.

"BY HOOK OR BY CROOK": **"To achieve something by any means possible".**
Originates from Mediaeval times when labourers were allowed to use the tools of their trade (**billhooks** for farm workers, **crooks** for shepherds) to snatch down twigs and branches from their Lords'/employers' trees to use for firewood.

i)"CARPETED" ii)"ON THE CARPET": i) Reprimanded ii) to be in trouble.
The expression comes from horse racing. Historically, Newmarket is known as the headquarters of British horse racing, and if someone had been accused and there was an enquiry, the person accused had to stand on a piece of **carpet** at the end of the table in front of the enquiry team at the Jockey Club's Newmarket headquarters. The Jockey Club is the organisation in charge of British horse racing.

CHAIRMAN: The most important person in a company/ organisation
When furniture was scarce, important people travelled with their own furniture which was usually a **chair**. Therefore, someone with a **chair** was an important person and **Chairman** became to mean the most important person in a company.

CHAIRMAN OF THE BOARD - tables were known as **Boards**, so the Chairman at the table/**board** was the most important person.

"COCK AND BULL STORY": An unbelievable, probably false story.
The town of Stony Stratford in Britain was a famous stop for coaches, with two famous coaching inns: **The Cock** and **The Bull**. Coach passengers would walk from one inn to another, their stories becoming more exaggerated as their alcohol intake increased.

DOLE: Someone **'on the dole'** is drawing Government money because they are out of work/unemployed.
The **Dole** Chest was a big chest usually kept in a church, where rich people put in bread to be handed or **'doled'** out to the poor.

DRAWING ROOM: The main reception room in a large house.
Originally called the **withdrawing room**, where the ladies withdrew to after dinner, leaving the men to get drunk on the bottles of Port they drank after dinner. The men would also to tell one another rude stories that were not fit for the ears of ladies.

"DRINK A TOAST": 'To raise drinking glasses and to drink the health of someone or something".
At one time a piece of **toast** was put into a glass of wine either to improve the flavour, or to collect the sediment. The word **'toast'**, thus, became identified with the drink.

DROVERS: Drovers were the parcel couriers of their day. These **couriers** used to herd geese and other animals to market, and also carry money to put in to banks for clients. They were so honest they were often commissioned to buy jewellery. They used tracks or dirt tracks to transport their goods, these tracks being often situated high above villages and valleys for security reasons.

DRY STONE WALLS: Hedges made of stones.
The **stones** that were used to make these **walls** were gathered from the fields and put to the side for collection. They are found in the Cotswolds, Lake District, Northumbria, and anywhere there were **slate-like limestone stones**. Some **walls** are over 800 years old. They are built on a broad base, narrowing up to a single **stone** at the top.

"FACE THE MUSIC": To confront an unpleasant event.
Originates from the days when, if a soldier had been dismissed from his Regiment, he was 'drummed out' when his 'wrong doings' were read out in front of the regiment. Whilst this was going on, the drums were beating.

"GILT ON THE GINGERBREAD": Adding something to make an event extra special.
On special days such as Saints' Days, **gingerbread cakes** were made more exciting by being covered with gold leaf and then sold as a special treat.

"GOD BLESS YOU"/"BLESS YOU": What you say when someone sneezes. Originates from the Middle Ages when sneezing was one of the first signs of the dreaded plague, and your friends called down **God's blessing** to protect you from the plague. - See Ring a Ring of Roses.

HUMPTY DUMPTY of the nursery rhyme was said to be Cardinal Wolsey, who fell from grace. **Humpty Dumpty 'had a great fall'** - when Cardinal Wolsey quarrelled with Henry VIII, he lost all his possessions. **Humpty Dumpty** was probably used as a reference to Cardinal Wolsey's physical stature.

"HUSH A BYE BABY": Is a nursery rhyme describing a baby rocking on the top of a tree. When the wind blows his cradle will rock, eventually sending baby, cradle and all tumbling down.
This describes the time when Mary of Modena, wife of King James II finally became pregnant. When her baby was born many people at Court swore that she hadn't been pregnant, but the baby had been smuggled into her bed in a warming pan-(mediaeval hot water bottle). King James was extremely unpopular, and William of Orange and his wife Mary had been invited to take over the throne. William was waiting in the Netherlands to come to England, but the winds were blowing in the wrong direction, so he could not sail to England. So the **baby's cradle rocked** the throne of England, and when the the wind finally blew in the right direction,William was able to land in England and take over the throne.

"KILLING THE GOOSE THAT LAYS THE GOLDEN EGGS": To grasp at more than you are due, and then to lose everything.
Greek legend says a farmer had a **goose that laid golden eggs** and the farmer thought that he would make himself rich by killing the **goose** expecting to get all

the **eggs** inside. By killing the goose and believing the greek legend, the farmer ended up with absolutely nothing.

"KNOCK UP": To wake up.
Originates from mining villages, where a slate hung beside the back door of houses. Miners would pay a small amount of money to the **'knocker upper'**; when the miners went to bed, they would write with chalk on the slate the time they wanted to be woken by the **knocker**. The **knocker** would tap on their window with a long pole at the time required. These slates can still sometimes be seen outside miners' cottages, particularly the row in Beamish Museum at Consett.

LADIES IN WAITING. Her Majesty the Queen, and certain female members of the Royal Family have **Ladies in Waiting** to help them with their official duties.
Legend has it that the term was given by Queen Elizabeth I; The Queen surrounded herself by pretty young girls who held honorary positions at Court as Maids of Honour. Their families would send them to Court to find husbands, and in return for food and lodging they would attend The Queen. One visitor, remarking on all the pretty Maids, was reputedly told by Queen Elizabeth that they weren't maids. So many of these pretty maids were pregnant that Queen Elizabeth called them all 'Ladies in Waiting'.

"LET YOUR HAIR DOWN": To enjoy oneself in an informal manner.
Originates from the time when young girls put their long hair up to show that they were grown up, mature adults.

When they were playing in private, they would **let their hair down** again.
MASTERPIECE: A very well-made object, painting or piece of furniture.
Originate from the time when boys were sent to a Craft Guild to learn a trade. The boys would make something to show their Guild Masters/ teachers. This 'something' was called a **Masterpiece** to show that they were able to become members of The Craft Guild, and that they were capable to work on their own.

"MURPHY'S LAW": "Whatever can go wrong, will go wrong".
In 1949 a man called Captain Murphy designed a harness to be worn by a test pilot to measure how much acceleration the human body could withstand. The test of the harness failed and the harness was blamed, but on examination, Captain Murphy found that a technician had wired the harness incorrectly for the test. Captain Murphy said that if **any technician can possibly do something wrong then he will.** This remark was overheard by a project manager and it was called **Murphy's Law.**

"ONE OVER THE EIGHT": To describe someone as having had too much alcohol to drink.
Originates from the time when officials at the Royal Court were allocated **eight pints of beer** to drink per day. Eight pints of beer was considered sufficient for one person and if people drank more, then they assumed as having had too much to drink and were, therefore, possibly drunk.

"PAY ON THE NAIL": To pay someone quickly.
Originates from Bristol when the Cap-

tains of ships would receive their pay from their employers by the 'pillars' or **'nails'** outside the Corn Exchange.

PEWS: Long, narrow wooden seats found in churches for people to sit on during church services.
When there were no seats in churches, people would stand during church services. When the Priest climbed into the pulpit to give his sermon, he would announce **'women and the weak, go to the wall**. At the walls of the church, there would be ledges for the women and the weak to sit, leaving the strong men to stand in the middle of the church. When **pews** were invented, they were very narrow, so if you fell asleep during the church service you **'DROPPED OFF'** the pew. This is where the phrase **'DROPPED OFF'** originates from, which means 'to sleep'

"PIG IN A POKE": To buy something **'blind'**, or to buy something ,when not actually knowing what you are really getting for your money.
Originates from the time when hop pickers carried a long **'poke' or sack** in which to put the hops when they had been picked. At agricultural markets and fairs, farmers would use these **'pokes' or sacks** to carry what they said was a **pig** to sell, but they were probably carrying a less expensive animal such as a cat. The farmers could hide this, because the **'poke' or sack** was so long. Buyers would trust the farmers and buy what they thought was a **pig** and therefore, **'buy a pig in a poke'**. When the buyers found out that they had actually bought a less expensive animal such as a cat, they found out the truth which is where the phrase **'TO LET**

THE CAT OUT OF THE BAG' originates from, **meaning 'to find out the truth'**

POST: Mail / Letter delivery
When letters were delivered by **mail** coaches travelling around Britain, the coachman would hang the sack of **letters/mail** on a **post** outside the towns and villages. A person from each of the towns and villages was paid to collect the sacks from the **posts** and they were called the **postman**

PUB SIGNS
By law, a pub (public house) has to have a **sign** outside stating its name, dating from the times when most people could not read. The pub signs would, therefore, have pictures as well as writing.

PUBLIC SCHOOLS : Private schools where parents pay for the education of their chilldren. Most are boarding schools where the children live during the academic term.
Originates from the days when the aristocrats and the gentry, who lived in castles and manor houses, wanted their sions to meet other boys, so sent them to **public** schools. The daughters of the aristocrats and the gentry stayed at home with their parents.

"PULLING THE WOOL OVER YOUR EYES": "To hide something from another person"
Originates from the time when **wigs** that were made of **wool** were worn by the most important people. If someone pulled the **woolen wig** down over these persons eyes, they would not be able to see.

"RAINING CATS AND DOGS": To rain very heavily.

In Norsk mythology, **cats** were supposed to have an influence over the weather, **dogs** were the signal of **wind** and were also the attendants of Odin who was the storm god. **Raining cats and dogs** thus meant, that the weather was a combination of the worst that cats and dogs could create together.

RED
i) "IN THE RED": To be overdrawn at the bank

When bank statements were hand written, if people were overdrawn at the bank, the balance would be written in **red ink** on the statement.

ii) "RED LETTER DAY": A day of celebration

Originates from the time when Saints' Days and festival days were written in **red ink** on calendars and diaries.

iii) "RED TAPE": Official rules and regulations.

Originates from the days when official documents and government papers were tied up and bound with **red ribbon.**

RING A RING OF ROSES, a pocket full of poses, atishoo! atishoo! we all fall down.

This nursery rhyme is told to children of all different nationalities all over the world. It probably dates from the time of the plagues: The **roses** were probably **circles of spots** that appeared as signs of the plague, **'Pocket full of poses'** reminds people of the time that people carried **bunches of sweet-smelling flowers and herbs** to protect people from 'evil influences', **'Atishoo':** sneezing was another sign of the plague, and to this day people all over the world

ask for Gods blessing when others sneeze, in order to give protection from the plague - **See 'God Bless You' / 'Bless You'.** Finally, **'we all fall down'** reminds us of all the people that died from the plague.

SACK
i) "TO SACK SOMEONE": To dismiss someone, usually from employment.
ii) "TO GET THE SACK": To be dismissed from employment.

The word **"sack"** originates from the days when boys training for employment used to carry the equipment necessary for their job in a **sack.** When they left the job, they used to take the **sack of equipment** with them.

SALT: In ancient times, salt was so important that Roman soldiers were paid their salarium - **salt money** (now salary). **The Saltcellar** was a large bowl, often ornamented and made of silver or gold in rich houses, and placed in the middle of the table. Important guests sat **'ABOVE THE SALT'** and unimportant guests sat **'BELOW THE SALT'.** If people spilt **salt,** it was said that it was probably the Devil who had jogged the person's arm, so people would **'THROW SALT OVER THE LEFT SHOULDER',** in order to hit the Devil in the eye.

"SIXES AND SEVENS": In a state of confusion.

This phrase dates from the time when two of London's Livery Companies (mediaeval Trade Union for employers) could not decide whether they were **sixth or seventh** in order of precedence and age. The two livery companies concerned were the Merchant Taylors and the Skinners. Both these companies received their Charters within a few days of each other in 1327, so in order to decide this problem, the two companies asked the Mayor and Aldermen to solve it. It was decided that each of the two livery companies should take alternative turns in taking precedence at processsions and dinners etc. This still happens to this day.

"SLEEP ON A CLOTHES LINE": When someone is so tired, they could sleep anywhere.
Originates from the time when poor travellers would sit down by the fire in an Inn/Pub because they could not afford to pay for a bed for the night. The wife of the owner of the Inn/Pub would often hang a **clothes line** across the chairs, so that the travellers could hook their arms over the **clothes line** and were, therefore, able to **sleep** without falling off the chairs.

STAMPS : British **stamps** are the world's oldest, so do not have the name of the country on them. Until Sir Rowland Hill had the idea for people to pay for letters as they were sent, people paid the postman when the letter(s) were delivered.

"TAKE SILK": When a well known barrister (member of the legal profession who works in the British High Court) is promoted to the Queen's Counsel, he or she are said **to'take silk'**. This comes from the thick **Ottoman silk** gowns that they wear after they have been promoted to become Judges and Counsel.

"TEA TOTAL": "non-alcoholic".
There are several explanations for the phrase **'tea total'**, but we will give only one explanation. Tea was a very expensive commodity and snobbish people liked their friends to know that they only drank tea in their homes and did not drink cheap beer. The house was , thus, **'tea total'**.

THATCHERS' MARKS: A **"thatch"** is straw or reeds that are used to cover the roof of a house or building. When **thatching** a house the **thatcher** will put his **mark**, like a signature, on top of the **thatch.** This is often an animal or bird

TIDDLY: "To be drunk".
Taken from cockney rhyming slang - **tiddlywink = drink**

"TO BE ON TENTERHOOKS": When someone's nerves are streched (to be nervous) or 'on edge', eagerly waiting for something to happen.
Originates from the days when cloth was woven, it was **stretched** on **hooks** passed through the **selvedge.**(The selvedge was the thick part of a piece of material/cloth used for attachment). This was called **'tentered'** which comes from the Latin word **'tentus' which means 'to stretch'**

"TURNING THE TABLES": "To get the better of someone"
Originates from the time when old furniture often served a dual purpose. There might be a **table** in a house, which would have a polished surface to impress neighbours and friends, When mealtime came, the surface was **turned over**, to reveal an unpolished surface underneath, on which a meal would be

served and eaten. It did not matter whether the unpolished side was damaged or dirtied. When the meal was finished, the surface was **turned over** again to reveal the polished, shiney surface.

"UNDER THE COUNTER": "Unlawful"
The expression comes from World War II when some shops kept/held rationed or scarce goods for their best customers, hiding them **under the shop counter**, so that the other customers could not see the goods.

"UPPER CRUST": "To be aristocratic or to come from the most important/ 'best' families"
Originates from when the top or **upper crust** of a loaf of bread was the **best** part